FOREIGN
LANGUAGES
PUBLISHING HOUSE
Moscow 1948

MINISTRY OF FOREIGN AFFAIRS OF THE U.S.S.R.

DOCUMENTS AND MATERIALS RELATING TO THE EVE OF THE SECOND WORLD WAR

VOLUME
I
November 1937-1938

*FROM THE ARCHIVES
OF THE GERMAN MINISTRY OF FOREIGN AFFAIRS*

Printed in the Union of Soviet Socialist Republics

PREFACE

In the early part of 1948 the State Department of the U.S.A. published a collection of reports and records of Hitlerite diplomatic officials under the title "Nazi-Soviet Relations, 1939-1941." One learns from the preface to this collection that in the summer of 1946 an agreement to publish German diplomatic documents was reached between the Governments of the U.S.A. and Great Britain. To this agreement France subsequently adhered. In 1945 the Soviet Government had addressed a proposal to the British Government that a joint study be made of the German documents and insisted that Soviet experts be allowed to participate. The Soviet Government's proposal was rejected. The American, British and French Governments undertook a separate publication of German documents, without the participation of the Soviet Union. In view of this, the Soviet Government feels entitled to make public the secret documents from the Archives of the German Ministry of Foreign Affairs captured by the Soviet Army on its triumphant entry into Berlin.

The documents included in the first volume of this publication relate to the period from November 1937 to December 1938. The volume comprises records of conversations of Hitler, Ribbentrop and other representatives of the German Government with foreign statesmen, reports of German foreign diplomatic representatives, and documents relating to the negotiations of the German Government with other governments, as well as documents of other governments having a direct bearing on the materials from the Archives of the German Ministry of Foreign Affairs contained in this volume.

The documents are arranged in chronological order. Notations of a routine and standard character customarily to be found on documents of this type are not reproduced in this publication, to wit:

1. Incoming file stamp. 2. Stamp indicating to which departments and officials of the Ministry copies were sent. 3. The stamps: "Geheime Reichssache" and "Geheimvermerk für Geheimreichssache." 4. No. of typed copy.

The nature of the document (letter, telegram, memorandum, etc.), is indicated, as well as its outgoing file number, and whether the document is marked secret or confidential. If the document in question is a copy, this is indicated.

Marginal notations of importance, and not merely of a routine nature, are reproduced. Where the translation is not from the German, but from some other language, this is indicated by footnotes.

The collection was prepared for the press by the Archives Department of the Ministry of Foreign Affairs of the U.S.S.R.

CONTENTS

Page

1. CONVERSATION BETWEEN HITLER AND HALIFAX, November 19, 1937 13

2. LETTER FROM GERMAN FOREIGN MINISTER NEURATH TO THE GERMAN MINISTER IN PRAGUE EISENLOHR, February 5, 1938 46

3. CONVERSATION BETWEEN HITLER AND HENDERSON, March 3, 1938 50

4. REPORT OF THE CZECHOSLOVAK MINISTER IN PARIS OSUSKÝ TO CZECHOSLOVAK FOREIGN MINISTER KROFTA, March 4, 1938 68

5. TELEPHONE CONVERSATION BETWEEN GOERING (BERLIN) AND RIBBENTROP (LONDON), March 13, 1938 . . . 81

6. TELEGRAM FROM THE GERMAN MINISTER IN PRAGUE EISENLOHR TO SECRETARY OF STATE IN THE GERMAN FOREIGN OFFICE WEIZSÄCKER, March 18, 1938 86

7. NOTE FROM THE BRITISH FOREIGN OFFICE TO THE SOVIET EMBASSY IN LONDON, March 24, 1938 89

8. LETTER FROM COUNSELLOR IN THE GERMAN FOREIGN OFFICE ALTENBURG TO THE MINISTER IN PRAGUE EISENLOHR, ENCLOSING MINUTES OF A CONFERENCE ON THE SUDETEN GERMAN QUESTION, PRESIDED OVER BY RIBBENTROP, March 29, 1938 93

9. LETTER FROM THE CZECHOSLOVAK MINISTER IN LONDON MASARYK TO CZECHOSLOVAK FOREIGN MINISTER KROFTA, April 5, 1938 100

10. STATEMENT BY MR. CHAMBERLAIN AT A MEETING OF BRITISH AND FRENCH MINISTERS, April 28, 1938 107

11. REPORT OF THE POLISH AMBASSADOR IN PARIS LUKASIEWICZ OF A CONVERSATION WITH THE FRENCH FOREIGN MINISTER BONNET, May 27, 1938 . . 109

12. REPORT OF THE GERMAN AMBASSADOR IN LONDON VON DIRKSEN TO THE MINISTRY OF FOREIGN AFFAIRS, July 10, 1938 122

13. CHURCHILL'S MEMORANDUM OF HIS CONVERSATION WITH THE HEAD OF THE DANZIG FASCISTS FOERSTER, July 14, 1938 135

14. LETTER FROM UNDER SECRETARY OF STATE IN THE GERMAN FOREIGN OFFICE WOERMANN TO THE GERMAN LEGATIONS IN BUCHAREST AND BELGRADE, July 25, 1938 139

15. REPORT OF THE POLISH AMBASSADOR IN BERLIN LIPSKI TO FOREIGN MINISTER BECK, August 11, 1938 145

16. MINUTE OF A CONVERSATION BETWEEN ASHTON-GWATKIN, COUNSELLOR TO THE BRITISH FOREIGN OFFICE AND THE LEADER OF THE NAZI SUDETEN GERMAN PARTY HENLEIN, August 22, 1938 156

17. HITLER'S ORDER FOR REPRISALS AGAINST CZECHOSLOVAKIA, September 15, 1938 . 163

18. MEMORANDUM OF VON STECHOW OF THE GERMAN FOREIGN OFFICE, September 15, 1938 165

19. LETTER FROM HIMMLER'S ASSISTANT BEST TO THE GERMAN FOREIGN OFFICE, September 19, 1938 167

20. LETTER FROM UNDER SECRETARY OF STATE IN THE GERMAN FOREIGN OFFICE WOERMANN TO HIMMLER, September 19, 1938 169

21. TELEGRAM FROM CZECHOSLOVAK FOREIGN MINISTER KROFTA TO CZECHOSLOVAK MINISTER IN PARIS OSUSKÝ . 171

22. BRITISH AND FRENCH PROPOSALS TO THE CZECHOSLOVAK GOVERNMENT, September 19, 1938 173

23. REPORT OF THE POLISH AMBASSADOR IN BERLIN LIPSKI TO FOREIGN MINISTER BECK, September 20, 1938 . . . 176

24. REPLY OF THE CZECHOSLOVAK GOVERNMENT TO THE ANGLO-FRENCH PROPOSALS, September 20, 1938 187

25. REPLY OF THE BRITISH GOVERNMENT TO THE CZECHOSLOVAK NOTE, September 21, 1938 191

26. LETTER FROM RUNCIMAN TO CHAMBERLAIN, September 21, 1938 193

27. MEMORANDUM OF THE CZECHOSLOVAK LEGATION IN MOSCOW TO THE PEOPLE'S COMMISSARIAT OF FOREIGN AFFAIRS OF THE U.S.S.R., September 22, 1938 203

28. TELEGRAM FROM UNDER SECRETARY OF STATE IN THE GERMAN FOREIGN OFFICE WOERMANN TO THE GERMAN DIPLOMATIC REPRESENTATIVES IN ROME, WARSAW, BUDAPEST, PRAGUE AND LONDON, September 23, 1938 205

29. MINUTE BY SMUTNÝ OF THE TRANSMISSION BY THE BRITISH MINISTER IN PRAGUE NEWTON OF HITLER'S DEMANDS ON CZECHOSLOVAKIA, September 23, 1938 211

30. TRANSMISSION OF HITLER'S DEMANDS ON CZECHOSLOVAKIA BY THE BRITISH MINISTER IN PRAGUE NEWTON, September 24, 1938. 215

31. FROM THE CZECHOSLOVAK MINISTER IN LONDON MASARYK TO BRITISH FOREIGN SECRETARY HALIFAX, September 26, 1938 217

32. REPORT OF THE POLISH AMBASSADOR IN BERLIN LIPSKI TO FOREIGN MINISTER BECK, September 26, 1938 . . . 219

33. REPORT OF THE POLISH AMBASSADOR IN BERLIN LIPSKI TO FOREIGN MINISTER BECK, September 27, 1938 . . . 226

34. COMMUNICATION OF THE GERMAN DELEGATION IN MUNICH TO THE GERMAN FOREIGN OFFICE ON THE COURSE OF THE MUNICH CONFERENCE, September 29, 1938 232

35. TEXT OF MUNICH AGREEMENT, September 29, 1938 244

36. KORDT'S MINUTE OF THE MUNICH CONFERENCE, September 29, 1938. 256

37. A CZECHOSLOVAK FOREIGN MINISTRY RECORD OF THE CZECHOSLOVAK DELEGATION'S VISIT TO MUNICH, September 30, 1938 264

38. TRANSMISSION OF THE MUNICH DEMANDS BY THE GERMAN CHARGÉ D'AFFAIRES IN PRAGUE HENCKE TO CZECHOSLOVAK FOREIGN MINISTER KROFTA, September 30, 1938. 268

39. ANGLO-GERMAN DECLARATION, September 30, 1938. 271

40. LETTER FROM KEITEL TO WEIZSÄCKER, October 10, 1938 272

41. TELEPHONE MESSAGE FROM GODESBERG TO SECRETARY OF STATE WEIZSÄCKER, October 12, 1938 276

42. FRANCO-GERMAN DECLARATION, December 6, 1938 284

43. MINUTE OF A CONVERSATION BETWEEN THE CZECHOSLOVAK FOREIGN MINISTER CHVALKOVSKÝ AND THE BRITISH MINISTER IN PRAGUE NEWTON, December 10, 1938 286

44. LETTER FROM THE POLISH AMBASSADOR IN LONDON RACZYŃSKI TO THE POLISH AMBASSADOR IN BERLIN LIPSKI, December 19, 1938 293

NAME INDEX 305

No. 1

CONVERSATION BETWEEN HITLER AND HALIFAX[1]

REICHSBANKPRÄSIDENT
Dr. HJALMAR SCHACHT[2]

Berlin, January 28, 1938

Received January 28, 1938
Reported to the Reichsminister [3]

Sehr verehrter Herr von Neurath,

Herewith I return the report of the visit of Lord Halifax and thank you for having let me see it.

Heil Hitler!
Yours faithfully,

Hjalmar Schacht

Reichsminister of Foreign Affairs
Freiherr von Neurath
Berlin
Ministry of Foreign Affairs

---

[1] Document from the Archives of the German Ministry of Foreign Affairs. Original.
[2] Letterhead.
[3] Stamp.

RECORD OF A CONVERSATION BETWEEN THE FÜHRER AND REICHSKANZLER AND LORD HALIFAX, IN THE PRESENCE OF THE REICHSMINISTER OF FOREIGN AFFAIRS, IN OBERSALZBERG,

November 19, 1937 [1]

Lord Halifax began by saying that he welcomed the opportunity to achieve a better understanding between England and Germany by means of personal talks with the Führer. This would be of the greatest importance not only for the two countries, but for all European civilization. Before leaving England he had discussed this visit with the Prime Minister and the British Foreign Secretary, and they were in full agreement as to its aims. The purpose was to ascertain how the opportunity could be arranged for a comprehensive and frank discussion of all questions

---

[1] Document from the Archives of the German Ministry of Foreign Affairs enclosed in Schacht's above letter to von Neurath of January 28, 1938.—*Ed.*

REICHSBANKPRÄSIDENT
DR. HJALMAR SCHACHT

BERLIN, DEN 28. Januar 1938.

Sehr verehrter Herr von Neurath !

           Anliegend gebe ich Ihnen mit bestem Dank für die Überlassung den Bericht über den Besuch von Lord Halifax zurück.

                                      Heil Hitler !
                                      Ihr ergebener

Herrn Reichsminister des Auswärtigen
Freiherr von N e u r a t h,
    Berlin
    . . . .
    Auswärtiges Amt.

Photostatic copy of Schacht's letter to Neurath of
January 28, 1938

Aufzeichnung über die Unterredung

zwischen dem Führer und Reichskanzler und Lord Halifax

in Anwesenheit des Herrn Reichsaußenministers

Am Obersalzberg am 19.11.1937.

Lord Halifax betonte eingangs, daß er die Gelegenheit begrüße, durch eine persönliche Aussprache mit dem Führer ein besseres Verständnis zwischen England und Deutschland herbeiführen zu können. Es wäre dies nicht nur für die beiden Länder, sondern auch für die gesamte europäische Zivilisation von größter Wichtigkeit. Vor seiner Abreise aus England habe er noch mit dem Premierminister und dem Englischen Außenminister über diesen Besuch gesprochen, und sie seien sich in der Zielsetzung absolut einig gewesen. Es handle sich darum, festzustellen, auf welche Weise die Gelegenheit für eine umfassende und freimütige Erörterung aller beide Länder betreffenden Fragen geschaffen werden könne. In England sei man der Auffassung, daß die zur Zeit bestehenden Mißverständnisse durchaus aus dem Wege geräumt werden könnten. Man erkenne die großen Verdienste, die sich der Führer um den Wiederaufbau Deutschlands erworben habe, voll und ganz an, und wenn die englische öffentliche Meinung zu gewissen deutschen Problemen gelegentlich eine kritische Stellung

x) it might no einnehme x), so liege dies zum Teil daran, daß man in Eng-
doubt be in
part because land nicht vollständig über die Beweggründe und Umstände
people in England
....

Photostatic copy of first page of the Record of Hitler's conversation with Halifax, November 19, 1937

affecting the two countries. It was the opinion in England that the existing misunderstandings could be completely removed. The great services the Führer had rendered in the rebuilding of Germany were fully and completely recognized, and if British public opinion was sometimes taking a critical attitude toward certain German problems, the reason might be in part that people in England were not fully informed* of the motives and circumstances which underlie certain German measures. The English Church, for instance, was following the development of the Church question in Germany with deep concern and uneasiness. Labour Party circles were likewise critical of certain things in Germany. ** In spite of these difficulties he (Lord Halifax) and other members of the British Government were fully aware that the Führer had not only achieved a great deal inside Germany herself, but that, by destroying Communism in his country, he had barred its road to Western Europe, and that Germany therefore could rightly be regarded

*it might no doubt be in part because people in England. . . . [1]

**In spite of these difficulties he (Lord Halifax) recognised that the Chancellor had not only performed great services in Germany, but also, as he would no doubt feel, had been able by preventing the entry of Communism into his

---

[1] The parallel passages in the margin are recorded in the original in the left-hand margin in English, the corresponding places in the German text to which they refer being indicated by asterisks.—*Ed.*

as a bulwark of the West against Bolshevism. The British Prime Minister held the view that it should be quite possible to find solutions by an open exchange of opinions. The solution even of difficult problems could be facilitated by mutual confidence. If Germany and Britain succeeded in coming, or even approaching nearer, to an understanding, it would, in the British view, be necessary that the countries which are politically close to Germany and England *should be brought into the discussions. He had in mind Italy and France, to whom it must be made clear from the beginning **that an Anglo-German rapprochement would not in any way be a manoeuvre hostile to Italy or France. There should not be the impression that the Berlin-Rome Axis or the good relations between London and Paris would suffer as the result of an Anglo-German understanding. After the ground had been prepared by an Anglo-German understanding, the four Great West-European Powers must jointly lay the foundation for lasting peace in Europe. Under no conditions should any of the four Powers remain outside this co-operation, or else there would be no end to the present unstable situation.

own country, to bar its passage further West. The Prime Minister held the view that it should be possible to find a solution of our differences by an open exchange of views.

*should be at the appropriate time brought into our discussions

**that an Anglo-German rapprochement would not mean an attempt to divide Berlin and Rome, any more than it would mean an attempt to divide France and England.

The Führer replied that an understanding between the four West-European Powers seemed to him very easy to arrange if it was just a matter of good will and mutual courtesy.

But it would be more difficult when it came to concrete fundamental problems. If Germany's co-operation is to be secured, then it must be asked how Germany will be regarded by the other partners—whether as a State in the sense of the Versailles Treaty, in which case it will hardly be possible to go beyond purely formal relations between the European countries. Or is Germany to be treated as a State which no longer carries the moral and material stigma of the Treaty of Versailles? In that case the logical conclusions must be drawn from this changed situation, because active co-operation in European policy could not be demanded of a State which was denied the warrant to act as a Great Power. The tragedy was that people in England and France still could not reconcile themselves to the thought that Germany, which after the Peace of Westphalia was for 250 years no more than a theoretical concept, had in the past fifty years become a reality.

It was the task of wise statesmanship to reconcile itself to this reality even if this should have certain unpleasant sides to it. The same was true of Italy and in a certain sense of Japan. History often creates realities which are not always pleasant. Germany had to put up with a reality of this kind, for Poland had not existed, so to speak, for more than 150 years, but now had been recalled to life. He (the Führer) considered it his chief task to educate the German people to put up with unpleasant political realities too. The essence of the problem to be discussed was, what active political co-operation could a country render which in other respects was denied the most urgent living necessities.

There were two possible ways of arranging relations between nations.

The free play of forces, which in many cases might mean active and drastic interference in the affairs of nations and might cause serious disturbances to our culture, which had been built up with such effort. The other way was, instead of the free play of forces, to permit the rule of "higher reason" (höhere Vernunft). It must, however, be realized that this higher reason must lead to roughly the same consequences as would result from the free play of forces. He (the Führer) had often asked himself in the past years whether mankind today was intelligent enough to replace the free play of forces by the method of higher reason.

In 1919 a great chance was missed to apply this new method. An unreasonable settlement was then preferred. Germany was thereby driven to take the course of the free play of forces, since this in the long run was the only way she had of securing the most elementary human rights. The future will depend on which of these two methods is chosen.

One must, when assessing the sacrifices which the method of reason is certain to claim here or there, try to visualize what sacrifices would result from a reversion to the old method of the free play of forces. It will then be clear that the former way is the cheaper.

Lord Halifax agreed with the Führer that purely formal relations were of little worth and that far-reaching agreement could be achieved only when all parties took the same stand and unity of views were attained. He, for his part, was also convinced that something durable could be achieved only on a real foundation, even if the realities involved were unpleasant to one or another party. He stressed that everyone in England looked upon Germany as a great and sovereign country, and only on this basis should negotiations with her be conducted. Britons were realists, and were perhaps more than others convinced* that the errors of the Versailles dictate must be rectified. Britain always exercised her influence in this realistic sense in the past. He pointed to Britain's role with regard to the evacuation of the Rhineland ahead of the fixed time, the settlement of the reparations problem, and the reoccupation of the Rhineland.[1] They must try to speak the same language, and refrain from indulging in loud talk, because this can only lead to misunderstandings and not make the problem any easier.

On the English side it was not thought** that the status quo must be maintained under all circumstances. It was recognized*** that one might have to contemplate an adjustment to new conditions,

* that mistakes had been made in the Treaty of Versailles which had to be put right.

** it was not necessarily thought

*** that one might have to contemplate an adjustment to

---

[1] In the original: "ebenso wie bei der Wiederbesetzung des Rheinlandes."—*Ed*.

new conditions, a correction of former mistakes and the recognition of changed circumstances when such need arose.

a correction of former mistakes and the recognition of changed circumstances when that became necessary. England exerted her influence only in the direction of preventing these changes from occurring by way of the unreasonable method to which the Führer referred, by the free play of forces, which, in the long run, implies war. He must once more stress, in the name of the British Government, that no possibility of changing the existing situation must be precluded, but that the changes must take place only on the basis of a reasonable arrangement. If both sides are agreed that the world is not static, then they must seek, on the basis of common ideals, to live up to this recognition in such a way as to direct the available energies in mutual confidence toward a common goal.

The Führer replied that he unfortunately had the impression that although the will was there to act in a reasonable way, there were big obstacles to reasonable solutions especially in the democratic countries, where political parties are in a position to exercise decisive influence on the actions of the government. He himself, in 1933-34, had made a number of practical proposals for the limitation of armaments, which if adopted would have saved Europe and the world a lot of money. These proposals were rejected one after another, although many statesmen were reasonable enough to realize that Germany could not remain for long in the position to which she had been reduced by the Versailles Treaty. But as political parties and above all the irresponsible press had a decisive influence on the decisions of governments, his proposals, such as for a 200,000-strong army, a 300,000-strong army, limitation of air armaments, were all rejected. The only result of his efforts to settle these questions was the naval agreement.

The situation was analogous today. Necessary reasonable solutions were frustrated by the demagogic line of the political parties. This was naturally a great difficulty. In contrast, he could point to the good relations he had established with Poland, in spite of the bad past. Yet Germany could not expect the least concession from other countries in regard to the satisfaction of her natural living requirements, because there the parties dominated. Germany was aware of the attitude of the parties in England toward the colonial question, especially the absolutely unfavourable attitude of the Conservatives. The same was the case in France. Germany could only take note of this attitude and recognize that under these conditions the colonial problem could not be settled. One had to wait. There were other instances when the demagogic attitude of the parties was the decisive factor instead of the statecraft of individual statesmen. Lithuania's seizure of the Memel region in 1923 and the subsequent treatment of Germany's protests was a striking example. That is why the majority of his proposals were rejected. In a way he was regarded by the parties in the democratic countries as a black sheep, and the mere fact that a proposal came from him was enough for it to be rejected. Today too the influence of the parties was being manifested in a similar way. It was a fact that some nations had not sufficient living space. If England with her 46 million inhabitants had to live solely off the home country, it would perhaps be easier for her to understand this. The prejudiced attitude toward the colonial question entirely came from the fact that it was considered self-understood that America and Russia should possess great territories, that

England should own one-quarter of the world, that France should have a colonial empire and that Japan should at least not be prevented from expanding. It was also considered self-understood that little countries like Belgium, Spain and Portugal should have colonies. Only Germany was told that under no circumstances must she have colonies. That characterized the attitude of the parties which, like the Conservatives in England, had taken an absolutely negative stand on the colonial question. What was the sense of inviting a country to positive co-operation, when in other matters it was denied the most primitive rights? Germany's behaviour in East Asia was criticized: it was declared to be a betrayal of the white race. Yet Germany remained faithful to the solidarity of the white race as against other races longer than any other country, and was criticized for her racial policy precisely by the democratic countries. Now she had given up all interest in East Asia. She might maintain business relations with this or that country. But since the German flag had vanished from East Asia, and since trade follows the flag, the business opportunities were in any event not very great.

International problems would be difficult to settle so long as political parties did not grow wiser, or forms of government were not established which did not allow these parties to exercise so much influence on the governments.

The Führer also pointed in this connection to the press interference in the matter of Lord Halifax's visit to Germany. He did not doubt that certain circles in England thought realistically. The naval agreement was a proof of that. But the decisive political factors, it seemed to him, held a different position. That at any rate was his impression after his nearly five years of government. He believed that any proposal he made would at once be torpedoed and that any government that wanted to accept it would meet with big difficulties from the opposition.

Lord Halifax replied that if the Führer was really of the opinion that no advance could be made on the road to understanding* so long as England was a democracy, further conversation could serve no useful purpose, for England would not change her present form of govern-

*Lord Halifax replied that, if the Chancellor was really of that opinion, it was clear that he had wasted his time in coming to Berchtesgaden and the Chancellor had wasted his time in receiving him. For if the Chancellor's premises were correct, it followed that no advance could be made on the road to understanding, and that, so long as England was a democracy, further conversation could serve no useful purpose.

*of what the Chancellor regarded as demagogic party manoeuvres. In the English view of[1] Government which was worthy of the name was under the domination of outside parties.

ment so soon. Nor was it correct to say that opportunities had been missed and offers rejected because of the influence of the political parties. This was definitely not true in regard to England. Offers were rejected because, rightly or wrongly, certain countries did not consider those offers a sufficient guarantee of security. The non-acceptance of such proposals was a proof of the principle that disarmament must follow security, and not the other way round. That England concluded the naval agreement with Germany, in spite of the fact that much in it was objectionable from the party standpoint, was proof that the British Government also acted independently of the parties. It was certainly not the slave* of demagogic party manoeuvres. In the English view no government which was worthy of the name should allow itself to be taken in tow by the parties. Nor was it correct to say that proposals had been rejected because the Führer—the "black sheep"— had made them. Some countries saw how Germany ignored treaty obligations for reasons that possibly were convincing to Germany, but

---

[1] Presumably "no."—*Ed*.

which were not very convincing to other countries. It was therefore only natural that German offers were scrutinized more critically in these quarters than might otherwise have been the case.

The British Government did not hold the view that the colonial question should not be discussed with Germany under any circumstances. It knows that it is a difficult problem. It was however clear that no British Government could discuss the colonial question with Germany isolated from other questions. It could only be considered as part of a general settlement which would restore tranquility and security in Europe.

Other interested countries must naturally be brought into the discussion of a general settlement. The Führer had referred to circles in England who were hostile to Lord Halifax's visit. *There were such hostile circles in other countries too. This however should not frighten those who wanted to build a better world political system.

The Führer replied that Lord Halifax had misunderstood him. Lord Halifax had proposed an agreement of the four Western Powers as the ultimate aim of Anglo-German co-

*Was he sure that the hostile circles were confined to England?

operation. Among them was France, and his remarks regarding the demagogy of the political parties applied primarily to France, of which they were probably one hundred per cent true. He had excluded England by referring to the naval agreement.

As regards the non-observance of treaty obligations, he remarked that other Powers had violated their treaty obligations before Germany, and only after all her proposals had been rejected did Germany resort to freedom of action. Even in the opinion of internationally recognized British jurists Germany had the right to demand the disarmament of other countries after she had fulfilled her treaty obligations in this respect one hundred per cent. She had also accepted the proposal of the late Prime Minister MacDonald regarding a 200,000-strong army. It was shipwrecked because of France.

In the colonial question, other countries had violated the Congo Act, which prohibited the carrying of war into African territory. Because she had trusted that the treaty would be observed by other countries, Germany had maintained only small military contingents in Africa.

Essentially, England and Germany had only one difference: the colonial question. It was a difference of views. If this could be eliminated, it was greatly to be welcomed. If not, then he (the Führer) could only regretfully take note of the fact. There were many spheres in which Germany and England had different views. But none of them had ever had any direct bearing on Anglo-German co-operation. In the matter of the colonies there were two opinions on the English side. The British Government declared that discussion was possible. The parties—and especially the Conservative Party—totally rejected the possibility of discussion. There were no other difficulties as between Germany and Britain.

Lord Halifax asked the Führer whether he thought it possible, in the event of a satisfactory settlement of the disputed questions, to bring Germany back into the League of Nations with a view to closer co-operation with other countries, and in what way the Covenant of the League of Nations should, in his opinion, have to be amended before Germany could rejoin it. Undoubtedly the good sides of the League were exaggerated by its overenthusiastic supporters. Nevertheless it must be admitted that the League stood for peaceful methods of settling international difficulties. If these methods could be realized in practice, this would bring us nearer to the second alternative which the Führer called, in contrast to the free play of forces, the "reasonable method." If the League were used in this way, *and the League was after all an international method, the details of which could perhaps be altered, it would have considerable effect upon the re-establishment of confidence between the nations. He therefore wanted to know the Führer's attitude toward the League of Nations, as well as toward disarmament. All other questions could be characterized as relating to changes in the European order, changes that sooner or later would probably take place. To these questions belonged Danzig, Austria and Czechoslovakia. England was only interested** that any alterations should be effected by peaceful evolution, so as to avoid methods which might cause far-reaching disturbances, which were not desired either by the Führer or by other countries.

*which was an international method

**it would have considerable effect upon the re-establishment of confidence between the nations.

. . . .

fell into the category of possible alterations in the European order which might be destined to come about with the passage of time.

. . . .
that any alterations should come through the course of peaceful evolution.

The colonial question was undoubtedly difficult. The British Prime Minister was of the opinion that it could be settled only by way of a new start and as part of a general settlement. He asked the Führer whether he could not give him a general outline of the solution of the colonial problem as he conceived it.

The Führer replied that in his opinion the fact that Germany was not a member of the League of Nations was not an Anglo-German problem. For America was not in the League either, yet no one would say that there were profound differences of views between England and America for this reason. Moreover, the League, because of the absence of Japan and the inactivity of Italy, was not a real League of Nations any longer. Whether Germany would ever return to Geneva was something that could not at the present time be said. She would certainly not return to a rudimentary League of Nations, nor would she enter a League which regarded it as its function to resist the natural development of political events and stood for the perpetuation of the existing state of affairs.

It would have been much more easy to settle the disarmament question earlier, because then the question was only one of limitation of armaments. Now England was herself arming on a scale never before witnessed in English history. Was England prepared to give up armament? He, the Führer, knew that the answer of the English side to this question was that, in arming, England was only making up for lost time. Germany was in a similar position. She too had to make good what she had failed to do in the past owing to too great a fidelity to treaties. She furthermore knew by experience that nations are weighed by the strength of their armaments, and she could see today that her weight in international affairs had been enhanced by her armament. The disarmament problem had become extremely complicated owing to the French alliance with Russia, which followed as a reply to certain German measures. The result was that Russia had been brought into Europe not only as a moral, but also as a weighty material factor, especially in consequence of her alliance with Czechoslovakia. Who, under these circumstances, could tackle the question of disarmament, and how was it to be done? He really therefore did not know how the settlement of the disarmament problem was to be undertaken. In any case, he was a fanatical foe of conferences, which were foredoomed to failure. In no circumstances would he permit himself to be persuaded by statesmen who must have a conference every three months to have any part in such undertakings. If the question of disarmament is to be tackled at all, it must be made clear from the beginning what is to be liable to disarmament. He referred to his earlier proposal to prohibit aerial bombing. Since the colonial powers regarded bombers as an effective means of breaking the resistance of refractory natives, they had rejected this proposal as contrary to their interests. In the light of the latest war experience in various parts of the world they were now even inclined to increase the number of their bombers.

Germany was arming, and she would not complain. She would observe her contractual obligations under the naval agreement, with the reservation, however, which was made by the German side at the time of the conclusion of the naval agreement, that Russia would not go in for unlimited naval armament. In that case a revision of the naval agreement would be necessary. He, however, did not have such a high opinion of Russian efficiency as to believe that such a contingency would arise in the foreseeable future.

If reasonable counsels prevailed a settlement could also be reached with Czechoslovakia and Austria. With Austria the treaty of July 11 had been concluded, and it was to be hoped that it would lead to the removal of all difficulties. It rested with Czechoslovakia herself to clear away the existing difficulties. All she had to do was to treat the Germans within her borders properly and then they would be quite satisfied. Germany herself was deeply interested in maintaining good relations with all her neighbours.

As to the colonial question, it was not for Germany to express any wishes. There were two possibilities. First, the free play of forces. What colonies Germany would take in this case could not be foretold. The second possibility was a reasonable settlement. Reasonable settlements must be based on right, in other words, Germany was entitled to her former possessions. When it was declared on all sides that international order must not be built on force but on right, he, the Führer, fully agreed. He would even be glad if the date from which this new order was deemed to operate were referred back to before 1914. Germany under the new arrangement would be extremely well off. He repeated that Germany saw no need to express any wishes with regard to colonies—she stood solely on the basis of right. It was for England and France to make proposals, if for any reason they thought the restitution of any particular German colony inconvenient. Germany's colonial demands were not prompted by imperial or military ambitions. It was not her intention to edge herself into any strategical line, she wanted colonies solely for economic reasons, as a source of supply of agricultural produce and raw materials. She was not eager to have colonies in areas where guns were liable to go off and where there was a great danger of international complications. If England, from strategical considerations, did not think it possible to return some territories, she could suggest compensation in other areas.

In any event Germany would not accept the Sahara as a colony, or territories in the Mediterranean, for she considered a position between two world empires a little too dangerous. Tsingtao and Kiaochow were also too exposed.

Foreign Minister Freiherr von Neurath said in connection with the question of the League of Nations that since Germany left the League she had never declined international co-operation whenever there was a prospect of practical action, and not just of talk. An illustration was Germany's collaboration on the question of non-intervention in Spain.

The Führer, on his part, referred likewise to the German-Polish and German-Austrian settlements and expressed the hope that a sensible solution could also be found with Czechoslovakia.

Lord Halifax replied that on some points he did not quite agree with the Führer, but he did not intend to go into them in further detail, because they concerned things which were not of decisive importance in the present talks.

Chamberlain and the British Government would be gratified if today's comprehensive and frank discussion were followed by further talks on individual questions between representatives of the two governments. It was regrettable that nothing followed Simon's and Eden's visit, and if this talk were to be followed by further negotiations it would make an extremely favourable impression on public opinion.

The Führer replied that he contemplated the continuation of the Anglo-German contact at first through diplomatic channels, for if the intention was to negotiate on concrete questions they would have to be carefully prepared beforehand. The chief reason for the failure of many similar negotiations in the past was lack of preparation. A conference could only come as the consummation of previous preparatory negotiations. It was clear to him that the most difficult issue was the colonial problem, about which the two sides were still very far removed from each other. England and France must make up their minds whether they were prepared to meet Germany's demands in general and in what direction. Germany could only make her demands known and hope that they would be given a reasonable reception.

After the lunch interval, Lord Halifax again reverted to the question of continuing the Anglo-German contact, and once more suggested direct negotiations between representatives of the governments. Such negotiations would not only be of value in themselves, but would also make a favourable impression on public opinion. There would be disappointment if these direct negotiations were postponed too long. Very much had been expected in England from the visit of the German Foreign Minister and there was great disappointment when in consequence of the "Leipzig" and "Deutschland" incident this visit could not take place. It would therefore be a good thing if further negotiations were now held between German and British representatives. There the colonial question could be discussed, and, he repeated, the British Government was quite ready to discuss this question. True, he must again add that any British Government could only examine the colonial problem as part of a general settlement. All the questions to be settled must be tackled simultaneously on a wide front.

The Führer replied that it was precisely negotiations on a wide front that required adequate preparation. In his opinion it would be better not to start discussions at all than to land in a situation where it had to be admitted that the results of the negotiations were unsatisfactory. It would be better to wait. Two such realistic nations as the German and the English should not allow themselves to be influenced by fear of a catastrophe. People were always saying that if this or that did not happen Europe would be heading for catastrophe. The only catastrophe was Bolshevism. Everything else could be settled. The mood of catastrophe was the work of an excited and malignant press. It was wrong to assert that the international situation today was exactly similar to what it was in 1912-14. Perhaps it would have been if there had not been the war with its lessons in the interval. He was not one of the politically nervous. A few years hence today's problems might perhaps look quite different. In a calmer atmosphere, after the situation in East Asia and Spain were cleared up, it would perhaps be easier to settle many things. If, therefore, one or other problem was at present too difficult, one might calmly wait two or three years.

The fateful thing was the role of the press. It alone was responsible for nine-tenths of the tension. The Spanish crisis and the alleged occupation of Morocco by German troops were examples which vividly illustrated the danger of irresponsible journalism. A direct premise for the pacification of international relations was therefore that all nations should co-operate in putting an end to journalistic filibustering.

Lord Halifax agreed with what the Führer had said about the dangers of the press. He also was of the opinion that the Anglo-German negotiations should be carefully prepared. Chamberlain had told him before he left that he would willingly take upon himself the risk that Lord Halifax's visit to Germany might be misrepresented in the press, provided this visit at least accomplished one step in the right direction. All that was needed was that both sides should have one aim in view, namely, the establishment and consolidation of peace in Europe.

Then Lord Halifax expressed his thanks for the opportunity for this talk and said that he would make a full and precise report of it to the British Premier. The Führer likewise expressed satisfaction at having had so frank and comprehensive a talk with Lord Halifax and said that he could fully accept on behalf of Germany the aim just mentioned by Lord Halifax. No one who, like him, had been a soldier in the world war wanted another war. Such too was the tendency in England and other countries. Only one country, Soviet Russia, stood to gain from a general conflict. All others were at heart in favour of the consolidation of peace.

No. 2

LETTER FROM GERMAN FOREIGN MINISTER NEURATH TO THE GERMAN MINISTER IN PRAGUE EISENLOHR[1]

Strictly Secret

Berlin, February 5, 1938
The German Legation, Prague
  By courier

Consideration has been given here lately to the question what role, if any, the treaty of arbitration concluded between Germany and Czechoslovakia in Locarno could play in the future development of relations between the two countries. These reflections were particularly prompted by your conversations with Messrs. Beneš and Krofta, as reported in your letter of December 21 last, No. A.III.1. General.[2] In this connection I would like to say the following:

When, at the time we occupied the Rhineland in March 1936, we denounced the Rhine Pact signed in Locarno, the question arose what repercussions we desired this action to have on the other parts of the Locarno Treaty linked with the Rhine Pact, to wit, the arbitration trea-

---

[1] Document from the Archives of the German Ministry of Foreign Affairs.

[2] Marginal note in blue pencil: Pol. II, 3431/37.—*Ed.*

ties with France, Belgium, Poland and Czechoslovakia. We then decided privately that the German-French and the German-Belgian arbitration treaties were to be regarded as having lost their validity along with the Rhine Pact, since these two treaties were so closely connected with the Rhine Pact that to treat them otherwise would be inherently contradictory. As to the arbitration treaties with Poland and Czechoslovakia, which are not linked so closely with the Rhine Pact, it was decided that they should be regarded as remaining unaffected by the Rhineland action, that is, as still continuing in force. The determining factor in this decision was the consideration that it was inexpedient unnecessarily to enlarge the circle of problems raised by our Rhineland action. Vis-à-vis the external world, namely, Poland and Czechoslovakia, this German standpoint was not expressed in any special notification, but by inferential action, in connection with the settlement of technical matters arising out of the two arbitration treaties. It so happened that in April 1936 the mandates of the neutral members of the Conciliation Commission set up under the German-Czechoslovak Arbitration Treaty, which are subject to renewal every three years, expired. The Czechoslovak Legation had suggested in a note verbale on February 18, 1936, that the mandates be prolonged for another three years. To this we replied in a note verbale on March 31, 1936, that is, after the Rhineland action, that we were agreeable to the proposed prolongation of the mandates. Similarly, in August 1937, we notified the Polish Government in a routine letter of the appointment of a new German member of the German-Polish Conciliation Commission, and, besides, in the course of German-Polish negotiations on Upper Silesian questions, we again made explicit reference to the Locarno Arbitration Treaty.

But, on the other hand, when the French Embassy, in a note verbale in May 1936, approached us on the question of renewing the mandates of the members of the German-French Conciliation Commission, the French Ambassador was orally informed that, in our opinion, with the nullification of the Rhine Pact, the German-French, as well as the German-Belgian, arbitration treaties "were likewise affected, and we therefore could not for the time being agree to the proposed renewal of the mandates." The French Embassy put in a written protest against this view, but we, nevertheless, stuck to our opinion. In reference to Belgium, this question has so far not been expressly discussed. Hence there is no doubt that Czechoslovakia can claim that we had recognized the validity of the German-Czechoslovak Arbitration Treaty even after the Rhineland action.

It should be borne in mind that the arbitration treaties with Czechoslovakia and Poland both impose the strict obligation to submit all disputed questions either to arbitration or to mediation. The political significance of this obligation is enhanced by the fact that, in the separate treaties they concluded among themselves at Locarno, France, Czechoslovakia and Poland expressly stipulated that any violation on the part of Germany of her obligations arising out of the arbitration treaties would be a casus foederis. Under these circumstances, the fact must not be lost sight of that if complications should arise between Germany and Czechoslovakia, the arbitration treaty may prove an inconvenient restriction on our freedom of action.

It might therefore be advisable to re-examine the question of the continued validity of the Czechoslovak Arbitration Treaty, and then, of course, also, of the German-Polish Arbitration Treaty. A certain argument in favour of this might be adduced from the fact that some of the stipulations of these treaties, although minor ones, are coupled with the League of Nations, and that Germany has recently, in her declaration of December 12 last, definitely refused to return to the League of Nations. With Poland we could probably reach an understanding without particular difficulty. In the case of Czechoslovakia, on the other hand, it is quite obvious that denunciation of the arbitration treaty would under present circumstances cause an international sensation and would be construed as preparation for active plans against Czechoslovakia, especially if, when denouncing the treaty, we gave it to be understood that we did not intend to conclude with Czechoslovakia a new arbitration treaty from which reference to the League of Nations would be omitted. For this reason such a step is at the present moment not contemplated here.

However, I consider it advisable, if in your talks the subject of the arbitration treaty should again be raised by the Czechoslovak side, that you should avoid any further acknowledgement of the continuing validity of this treaty and, in general, should avoid assessing it as an essential factor in the relations between the two countries. It would do no harm if you were casually to remark at a convenient opportunity that in your personal opinion, owing to the collapse of the Locarno system and Germany's definite repudiation of the League of Nations, treaties such as the German-Czechoslovak treaty of arbitration have lost their political foundation.

I intend to discuss our further position in this matter with you personally the next time you come to Berlin.

Signed: ***Neurath***

No. 3

CONVERSATION BETWEEN HITLER AND HENDERSON[1]

MINUTE
OF A CONVERSATION BETWEEN THE FÜHRER AND
REICHSKANZLER AND HIS BRITANNIC MAJESTY'S
AMBASSADOR, IN THE PRESENCE OF REICHSMINISTER
OF FOREIGN AFFAIRS VON RIBBENTROP,

On March 3, 1938, in Berlin

The British Ambassador began by stressing the confidential nature of the conversation. Nothing regarding the subject of the talks would be divulged to the French, and still less to the Belgians, Portuguese or Italians. They would only be told that the conversation was a sequel to the talks between Lord Halifax and the Führer and related to questions concerning Germany and England.

He, Henderson, wanted, on the one hand, to set forth in broad outline an attempt at a solution suggested by the British Government, and if possible to hear the German view from the Führer. He pointed out that he was speaking only for the British Government, which wanted to have a clear idea of the situation before getting into

[1] Document from the Archives of the German Ministry of Foreign Affairs. Copy.

contact with other Powers for the realization of its proposals. In relation to third Powers, therefore, this conversation must be confidential.

Furthermore, he had to stress that this was not a commercial deal but an attempt to establish a basis for genuine and cordial friendship with Germany, beginning with an improvement of the atmosphere and ending with the creation of a new spirit of friendly understanding. Without underrating the difficulties to be overcome, the British Government believed that the moment was favourable for such an attempt to improve mutual relations. But the attempt was bound to fail if both sides did not contribute to the effort to reach agreement, in other words, if agreement were to be achieved, it could only be on a basis of reciprocity. Germany's positive contribution was needed for the establishment of tranquility and security in Europe. As was already made clear in the course of the Halifax conversation, instead of the free play of forces, a solution dictated by higher reason must be found. Lord Halifax had already admitted that changes in Europe were to be regarded as quite possible, but these changes must follow the lines of the aforesaid higher reason. The purpose of the British proposal was to contribute to such a reasonable settlement.

After the British Ambassador had made these personal observations, he proceeded to communicate his instructions. He stated that, on the instructions of his Government in London, in conversations with Prime Minister Chamberlain and other interested members of the Cabinet, he had examined all the questions that had arisen in connection with Halifax's visit to Germany. He stressed in this connection the importance of German co-operation in the tranquilization of Europe, to which he had already referred in earlier conversations with Herr von Neurath and Herr von Ribbentrop. Such tranquilization could be furthered by limitation of armaments and by appeasement in Czechoslovakia and Austria. In connection with this the British Ambassador orally communicated the following instructions, which he then transmitted in written form:

"In the opinion of the British Government, mutual appeasement will depend, among other things, upon measures undertaken with the object of creating confidence in Austria and Czechoslovakia. The British Government is not yet in a position properly to assess the consequences of the agreements recently reached between Austria and the German Reich, and these consequences must necessarily depend on the manner in which both parties implement the various obligations and arrangements. The British Government is therefore still in doubt as to how these agreements will influence the situation in Central Europe, and it cannot overlook the fact that the latest developments have caused concern in many quarters, which will unavoidably hamper a general settlement."

In reference to limitation of armaments, Henderson remarked that the British Government was of course aware of the difficulties, and he recalled the Führer's proposal to ban aerial bombing. The British Government would gladly welcome such a proposal. But what it considered even more important was to limit bomber aircraft in general. Taking into consideration the German proposals made two years ago, the British Government was again studying the whole set of questions here involved and hoped to be able to make acceptable proposals. It would be interesting to hear the German attitude toward this question.

In reference to the colonies, the British Ambassador stated that the British Government was earnestly prepared

Aufzeichnung

über die Unterredung zwischen dem F ü h r e r und
Reichskanzler und dem Königlich B r i t i s c h e n
Botschafter in Anwesenheit des Herrn Reichsministers
des Auswärtigen von R i b b e n t r o p am 3.März 1938
in Berlin.

Einleitend unterstrich der Britische Botschafter den vertraulichen Charakter des Gesprächs. Den Franzosen und noch viel weniger den Belgiern, Portugiesen oder Italienern würde irgend etwas über den Inhalt der Aussprache mitgeteilt werden. Es würde ihnen nur gesagt, daß dieses Gespräch sich in Verfolg der Besprechungen zwischen Lord Halifax und dem Führer mit den Deutschland und England angehenden Fragen befaßt habe.

Er, Henderson, wolle einerseits in großen Linien einen Lösungsversuch der Englischen Regierung vortragen und, wenn möglich, die deutsche Ansicht vom Führer dazu entgegennehmen, wobei er darauf hinweise, daß er nur für die Englische Regierung spreche, die bevor sie mit anderen Mächten über die Durchführung ihrer Vorschläge in Fühlung trete, zunächst einmal für sich selbst die Lage klären wolle. Daher müsse das Gespräch auch dritten Mächten gegenüber vertraulich behandelt werden.

Außerdem sei zu betonen, daß es sich um kein Handelsgeschäft handle, sondern um einen Versuch, die Grundlage für eine wahrhafte und herzliche Freundschaft zu Deutschland her-

not only to examine the colonial question, but also to make an advance toward its settlement. Prime Minister Chamberlain was personally dedicating all his attention to this question. Here, too, of course, the difficulties were great, since twenty years had elapsed since the last rearrangement of colonial possessions. Besides, public opinion in England was particularly sensitive on this point. The British Ambassador then read the following proposal on the colonial question, which he transmitted in writing at the end of the conversation:

"A solution which in the opinion of the British Government would have many advantages would be to work out a plan based on a new regime of colonial administration in some given part of Africa: this plan should embrace an area roughly equal to the Congo Basin, and should be accepted and applied by all the interested Powers. Each of them, although it would be alone responsible for the administration of its own territories, would be called upon to guide itself by certain principles designed to further the general welfare.

"Here, for example, the question of demilitarization would arise, both for the welfare of the natives and for the sake of freedom of trade and communication. It might also be that a commission composed of representatives of all the Powers owning parts of the given territory would be set up."

In reading this proposal, he mentioned that the territory in question would be bounded in the north roughly by the 5th parallel, and in the south roughly by the River Zambezi, and added that a commission would probably be set up composed of the Powers whose colonial possessions were situated within this area. He concluded by asking the Führer

1) whether Germany was prepared in principle to

participate in a new colonial regime as contemplated in the British proposal, and

2) what contribution she was prepared to make toward general tranquility and security in Europe?

The Führer replied that the most important contribution to the establishment of tranquility and security in Europe would be to ban the international inflammatory press, because nothing menaced security more than the intrigues of this press, which was unfortunately widely represented in Britain too. He pointed out that he personally was known to be one of the warmest friends of England, but that his friendship had been evilly repaid. Nobody perhaps was more often or more bluntly repulsed by England than he. It was therefore understandable that he had now withdrawn into a certain isolation, which seemed to him more dignified than to offer himself to those who did not want him and were constantly rejecting him.

To the objection of the British Ambassador that this rejection came only from certain circles in England, the Führer rejoined that the British Government must have been in a position to influence the press to adopt a different tone. Germany had information from friends in England that the press was influenced by the highest quarters in taking the trend in question, consequently the primary thing was that the inflammatory press campaign must cease.

In reference to Central Europe, he had to remark that Germany would not allow third Powers to interfere in the settlement of her relations with kindred countries or countries with large German populations, just as it would not enter Germany's head to interfere in the regulation of Anglo-Irish relations. The thing, therefore, was to prevent the continuation or resumption of an injustice toward millions of Germans. In this attempt at regulation, Germany must declare with all seriousness that she will not consent to allow this regulation to be in any way influenced from any other quarter. It was impermissible that on the one hand freedom of nations and the democratic rights should be always represented as elements of the European order, but that the very opposite should be asserted when it was a question of improving the lot of the Germans in Austria, where a government, which came into being not in a legal way, as the German Government had, and which had only 15 per cent of the population behind it, was oppressing the other Germans. Such a situation could not continue for long, and if England continued to oppose the German effort to achieve a just and reasonable settlement here, then the moment would come when it would be necessary to fight. When he, the Führer, was striving, as he had done at Berchtesgaden, to lighten the lot of the oppressed Germans by peaceful means, yet Paris and London not only treated his efforts sceptically, but instructed their diplomats to hinder the accomplishment of these peaceful attempts (here the British Ambassador interjected that England had never done so), they were rendering a very poor service to peace. After all, in order to achieve a satisfactory settlement, in Austria the people themselves should be asked, and in Czechoslovakia the Germans must be granted the autonomy to which they are entitled both culturally and in other respects. This would be the most elementary application of that right to self-determination of nations which figured so largely in Wilson's fourteen points. At any rate, the present situation could not continue for long, it would lead to an explosion, and it was in order to avoid this that the agreements were concluded in Berchtesgaden, and it might be said that the difficulties might be regarded as removed if the Austrian Government carried out its promises. Those who, on the contrary, apply force against reason and right, call force into the field, as he had already said in his speech in the Reichstag.

In reply to an inquiry from the British Ambassador whether Germany demanded a plebiscite in Austria, the Führer said that what was required was that by the road of evolution the legitimate interests of the German Austrians were guaranteed and the oppression ceased.

The British Ambassador stated that the present British Government had a keen sense of reality. Chamberlain had taken over the leadership of the people, instead of allowing himself to be led by the people. He had displayed great courage when, heeding nothing, he unmasked such international phrases as collective security and the like. It was difficult to find in history two men who not only wanted the same thing, but were moreover determined to achieve it at one and the same moment. England therefore declared her readiness to remove all difficulties and asked Germany whether she was prepared, on her part, to do the same.

The Führer referred to the proposals he had made some years ago. The reply was the Franco-Russian pact, which, when it was joined by Czechoslovakia, became particularly dangerous to Germany, because it constituted a grave menace to the industrial regions on the Reich's frontiers, in the Ruhr and in Saxony, and the enemy was always in a position to strike at the very heart of Germany. It was therefore necessary on the German side to take thorough measures of defence against this encirclement. Consequently, the limitation of armaments in a large degree hinged on Soviet Russia. What was to be expected from that quarter was recently made clear in a speech by Voroshilov, in which it was announced that the Soviet armed forces would not hesitate to use poison gases. Germany must be armed against this. The problem was especially complicated by the fact that one could no more rely on so barbaric a creation as the Soviet Union observing treaty obligations than on a savage understanding mathematical formulas. Agreements with that country would therefore be as good as worthless. Soviet Russia should not have been allowed into Europe. He, the Führer, when he made his proposals had had in mind a union of Europe without Russia.

Asked by the British Ambassador whether Germany would join in a ban of aerial bombing, the Führer replied that he had long ago made known his attitude toward this question, and could only add today that Germany would no longer allow herself to be deceived by empty promises, as had been the case with Wilson's fourteen points. Even if the Soviet Union were to declare today that it no longer intended to drop poison gas bombs, no faith could be placed in such a declaration.

To the objection of the British Ambassador that the question at this moment was solely one of the relations between England and Germany, the Führer replied that England had no trouble to fear from Germany, that Germany was not interfering in Empire affairs. But it had been her experience that whenever she endeavoured to solve her difficulties England reacted negatively. When an attempt is made to find a solution in the East, the British "No!" is to be heard just as it is when colonies are demanded, and everywhere the British press stands in the way of Germany and conducts a campaign of calumny against her.

The British Ambassador replied that the blame for the appearance of false news in the press lay not only with the British side: the working of the German press censorship was the cause of the origin of many false reports, and furthermore there had been strong attacks on England in the German press, especially at the time he had entered on his duties.

In answer to this the Führer pointed out that for three years, from 1933 to 1936, absolute silence had been maintained in Germany in face of all the British attacks. But, while Germany had never interfered in Britain's affairs, in Ireland, etc., there were continuous attempts at interference from the English side, by the bishops, by certain Members of Parliament, and by others.

In this connection the British Ambassador mentioned in confidence that Lord Halifax had today appointed a press conference of responsible newspaper editors, and had also had a talk with the president of the Newspaper Proprietors' Association and leading officials of the BBC, in the course of which he had again emphasized their responsibility in the maintenance of peace. In view of British freedom of the press, more than this could not be done. It was worthy of note, however, that the new British Foreign Secretary, who on the basis of his talks in Germany was fully informed of the German viewpoint, had here, as in other matters, already exercised his influence very considerably, by means of the British way of personal contact. In order to illustrate that on the German side too there were misapprehensions about conditions in England, the British Ambassador instanced the false opinion in Germany that the Vansittart Committee was behind the wave of anti-German propaganda. He could affirm on his word of honour that this Committee had nothing to do with the false reports. It was in general not an instrument of propaganda against any country; its purpose rather was to win sympathy for Britain and the British world empire.

Reichsminister of Foreign Affairs von Ribbentrop pointed in this connection to Reuter's two weeks' lie campaign. No one responsible for the false reports was dismissed or even reprimanded. There must be a system behind it.

The Führer took note of the reiterated assurance of the British Ambassador (the latter had declared that the Committee had not yet really begun to function) regarding the Vansittart Committee and, summing up, said that if the tension was to be relieved, the decisive thing was that the press should be better instructed, that the inflammatory reports should cease and an attitude of greater objectivity adopted.

To a question from the Führer regarding the new colonial regime, the British Ambassador, pointing to a map, replied that the British Government envisaged a system with principles similar to those of the Berlin agreement of 1885 (this presumably refers to the Congo Act). The colonies in this region of Africa would be redistributed. Germany would be considered in this redistribution, and would therefore have a colonial possession under her sovereignty. All the Powers possessing colonies in this Central African territory would however have to assume definite obligations in respect to demilitarization, freedom of trade and treatment of the natives.

The Führer replied that, naturally, Germany was above all interested in what was to happen to her former colonies. Instead of setting up a complicated new system, why not settle the colonial question in the simplest and most natural way, namely, by restoring to Germany her former colonies? True, he, the Führer, was bound to admit openly that he did not think that the colonial question was ripe for settlement, since Paris and London were too firmly committed not to restore the colonies. He therefore did not want to press the matter. One could calmly wait four, six, eight or ten years. Perhaps by then a change of mind will have taken place in Paris and London, and it will be seen that the best solution would be to restore to Germany the property she had lawfully acquired by purchase and treaty. The premise for Germany's co-operation in a new colonial regime was therefore the restitution of her former colonies, which had been lawfully acquired, and which had been taken away from her by the treaty. Germany did not want to burden countries which were not involved with the settlement of the colonial question. Perhaps also Belgium and Portugal would not consent, and perhaps they might think that Germany was demanding something from them to which she was not entitled.

The British Ambassador once again explained the British colonial plan on the globe, and, in reply to a question from the Führer, Sir Nevile Henderson declared that he believed Portugal and Belgium and, in the long run, France and Italy would participate in the settlement.

The conversation then reverted to the Central European problems and, in reply to the remark of the British Ambassador that Chamberlain could achieve something only if Germany made her contribution, the Führer replied that the Berchtesgaden agreement with Austria was to be regarded as his contribution to this matter, but that he must however declare with all emphasis that if ever Germans in Austria or Czechoslovakia were fired on, the German Reich would be on the spot.[1] He, the Führer, had had to do much talking in the course of his political career, and therefore perhaps certain circles believed that his words were not always to be taken too seriously. But those who thought

---

[1] In the original: "das Deutsche Reich dann zur Stelle sein würde."—*Ed.*

that his statements on the Central European questions were pure rhetoric were cruelly deceived. If explosions from within were to occur in Austria or Czechoslovakia, Germany would not remain neutral but would act with lightning speed. It was therefore a mistake for certain diplomats or certain quarters to tell the Vienna Government that it had nothing to fear, and that it need not carry out its obligations to the letter.

Reichsminister of Foreign Affairs von Ribbentrop here drew attention to the dramatic conversation between the British Minister in Vienna and Herr von Papen, in the course of which the Minister heatedly complained of the pressure Germany had allegedly exerted on Austria. The pressure at Berchtesgaden consisted solely in the fact that Austria's attention was drawn to certain dangers, and a means of eliminating them was envisaged. If the British Minister protested in such a dramatic way to Herr von Papen, then how must he have talked to Austrian Foreign Minister Schmidt.

The British Ambassador said that the statements of the Minister did not necessarily represent the views of the British Government, and declared that he, Sir Nevile Henderson, had often expressed himself in favour of the Anschluss.

The Führer replied to this that there were certain things which were simply unbearable for a Great Power. England declared that she could not tolerate an attack upon Belgium or Holland. He, the Führer, must declare with equal emphasis that if Germans continue to be oppressed in Central Europe in the same way or by other methods, Germany must and will interfere.

The British Ambassador summed up the German standpoint with regard to Austria and Czechoslovakia as meaning that if the Germans in those countries continue to be oppressed an explosion would follow, and that, on the contrary, if full equality were granted, no conflict was to be expected.

On the question of the limitation of air armaments the Führer remarked that disarmament naturally could not be undertaken only in definite parts of the world, since the air arm was extremely mobile. For instance, an air force from the Far East could easily be employed in Europe. Territorial limitations were therefore not to be considered. He, the Führer, when he made his earlier proposals, had been guided by the thought that the Geneva Convention forbade war against non-combatants. Unfortunately his proposals were not accepted. The British Ambassador replied that it was true that formerly the British Government would not hear of a prohibition of bombing, but that it now took a different stand, and, in conclusion, he added that for various reasons the present moment was favourable for talks concerning armaments. Germany was strong, but England too was again strong. Germany had awakened England out of her slumber, so that neither of the two negotiating parties could assume that the talks were prompted by fear or weakness. He, the Ambassador, shared General Field-Marshal Goering's view that only negotiations between the strong promise to be fruitful. On the other hand, a lot of money was being spent on armaments, so that from this point of view too there was an incentive to limitation.

The Führer replied that German armament was made necessary by Russia. It was a matter of life and death to Germany to protect her position in Central Europe, and she must arm against an attack by Soviet Russia, which naturally could never be checked by the Border States or by Poland. Hence, when talking of armament, the British should begin with Russia.

Deutschland habe England aus seinem Schlummer geweckt, sodass keiner der beiden Verhandlungspartner annehmen könne, die Verhandlungen fänden aus Furcht oder Schwäche statt. Er, der Botschafter, sei mit Generalfeldmarschall Göring der Ansicht, dass nur Verhandlungen zwischen Starken aussichtsreich seien. Andererseits würde viel Geld für Rüstungen ausgegeben, sodass auch in dieser Hinsicht ein Interesse an der Begrenzung bestünde.

Der Führer erwiderte, dass die deutsche Rüstung durch Russland bedingt sei. Für Deutschland sei es eine Lebensfrage, seine Position in Mitteleuropa zu verteidigen, und es müsse sich für einen Angriff von Sowjetrussland, der durch die Randstaaten und Polen niemals natürlich aufgehalten werden könne, wappnen. Bei einem Rüstungsgespräch müssten die Engländer daher zunächst bei Russland beginnen.

Auf eine erneute Frage des britischen Botschafters nach der deutschen Stellungnahme zum englischen Kolonialvorschlag stellte der Führer wegen der Wichtigkeit der Frage eine schriftliche Antwort in Aussicht.

Auf die Frage des Reichsaussenministers von Ribbentrop, ob die Rückgabe *aller* ehemaligen Kolonien, auch derjenigen, die im Besitze britischer Dominien seien, von der englischen Regierung in Auge gefasst werden könne, erwiderte der Britische Botschafter, dass er nur für Grossbritannien sprechen könne und seine Ausführungen sich nicht auf die Dominien bezögen.

gez. Dr. Schmidt
Legationsrat.

Hiermit dem Reichsaussenminister
von Ribbentrop
weisungsgemäss vorgelegt.
Berlin, den 3. März 1938.

Photostatic copy of last page of Document No. 3

To the repeated question of the British Ambassador regarding Germany's attitude toward the British colonial proposal, the Führer, in view of the importance of the matter, promised to give an answer in writing.

Asked by Reichsminister of Foreign Affairs von Ribbentrop whether the British Government could contemplate the restitution of *all*[1] the former colonies, including those now in the possession of British dominions, the British Ambassador replied that he could only speak for Great Britain and that what he said did not refer to the dominions.

Signed: *Dr. Schmidt*

Legationsrat [2]

---

[1] Underscored in the original.—*Ed.*

[2] There is a notation at the foot of the original document: "Submitted to Reichsminister of Foreign Affairs von Ribbentrop, according to instructions. Berlin, March 3, 1938.—*Ed.*

No. 4

REPORT OF THE CZECHOSLOVAK MINISTER IN PARIS OSUSKÝ TO CZECHOSLOVAK FOREIGN MINISTER KROFTA[1]

Ministry of Foreign Affairs   *Secret*
Office of the Minister   Political Archives[2]
No. 1095/38

Translation of a Letter of the Czechoslovak Legation in Paris
Legation of the Czechoslovak
Republic in Paris

         No. 229/38—*Confidential*

Paris, March 4, 1938
Confidential[3]

Dr. Kamil Krofta,
Minister of Foreign Affairs, Prague

Re: French Parliament
and Foreign Policy

         Mr. Minister,

Conflict of Two Political Trends

I have waited for the meeting of the Senate Foreign Affairs Committee, which was appointed for Wednesday,

---

[1] This document was seized by the Germans in the archives of the Czechoslovak Ministry of Foreign Affairs and translated by them into German. The document in the possession of the Archives Department of the Ministry of Foreign Affairs of the U.S.S.R. is the German translation found in the files of the former German Ministry of Foreign Affairs.—*Ed.*

[2] Stamp.

[3] This word is struck out in red pencil and corrected to "Secret" (Geheim). The correction was made in the German Ministry of Foreign Affairs to the German translation of the document.—*Ed.*

March 2, before giving you a general idea of the debate on foreign policy in the French Chamber of Deputies. I wanted to wait and see whether, and in what manner, the debate in the Senate Foreign Affairs Committee would supplement or correct the declarations made in the Chamber on February 26.

After the events in Austria following on the meeting in Berchtesgaden, the Czechoslovak question[1] came to the forefront. I will not conceal from you that in Paris people of diverse professions and walks of life—not excluding journalists and members of parliament—have begun to give form and expression to their resistance to the thought that France may have to go to war with Germany over Czechoslovakia. Under the influence of Eden's resignation, both the supporters of an understanding with Germany and the supporters of an understanding with Italy, as well as the opponents of France's policy in Central Europe and of her policy towards Russia, wanted to make an attempt to reorientate French policy. It must be realized that Eden's resignation made such an impression in Paris, that public opinion and the Government itself were deeply disturbed by it. Former Prime Minister and Foreign Minister Pierre Étienne Flandin raised the standard on behalf of a reorientation of French policy. On the other side, the Communists, the supporters of a military alliance with Soviet Russia, and those who are convinced that war is inevitable and that therefore all the forces of the nation must be organized, wanted to take advantage of the opportunity and definitely destroy all possibility of an agreement with Berlin and Rome. Besides the Communists, this policy was pursued by Paul Reynaud. He publicly advocated an all-round military alliance[2] with Russia; for which reason he also insisted

---
[1] In the German text the word "question" (Frage) is inserted in ink above the line.—*Ed*.

[2] In the original: "absolutes wie militärisches Bündnis."—*Ed*.

on the participation of the Communists in the Government. He considerably damaged the effectiveness of his policy by two considerations: 1) by assuming and asserting that war was inevitable, and 2) by saying that a military alliance must be concluded with Soviet Russia. Because the French people were scarcely likely to wax enthusiastic over a policy which presumed the inevitability of war, and, furthermore, the Right, the Centre and a large section of the Radicals consider the entry of the Communists into the Government unacceptable. Under these circumstances, Flandin's followers and Flandin himself believed that the moment was psychologically ripe for a French political reorientation. Flandin made a tour of his constituency and talked with peasants in the market places, asking them expressly whether they were prepared to go to war on behalf of Czechoslovakia. The answer to a question put in this way was naturally in the negative. This strengthened his conviction that the situation was ripe. Paul Reynaud, on the other hand, did not think of the peasants, and based his judgment of the situation on the mood of the workers. That is why he committed an error in so ardently advocating the participation of the Communists in the Government.

Minister Delbos[2] State of Mind

Minister Delbos is terribly tired and extremely fearful. What he would like most is not merely to quit his post, but to simply run away, if he only knew how. He is afraid of any idea that has a definite colouring; all colours hurt his eyes and his feelings. He composed his speech himself, but what he composed was quite colourless. It was his subordinates, Léger, Massigli and Rochat, that propped up his spirits and forced him to speak somewhat more colourfully. As to Czechoslovakia, I have already told you the most essential in my code message No. 13, in reply to your No. 8.

Ministerium für Auswärtige Angelegenheiten
Kabinett des Herrn Ministers, Nr. 1095/38.

Geheim
z. Pol. Arch.

Übersetzung eines Schreibens der Tschecho-slowakischen Gesandtschaft in Paris.

Gesandtschaft der Tschechoslowakischen
Republik in Paris.
Nr. 229/38 - Vertraulich.

Paris, den 4. März 1938.

Betr.: Das französische Parlament und die Außenpolitik.

Vertraulich.

Dieser Vermerk ist mit Rotstift gestrichen und in „Geheim" geändert.

Herr Minister !

Das Ringen zweier politischer
Strömungen.

Ich habe die für Mittwoch, den 2. März, einberufene Versammlung des Senatsausschusses für Auswärtige Angelegenheiten abgewartet, um Ihnen ein Gesamturteil über die Aussprache über die Außenpolitik im französischen Abgeordnetenhause geben zu können. Ich wollte abwarten, ob und in welchem Sinne die Aussprache im Auslandsausschuß des Senats die Erklärung im Abgeordnetenhaus vom 26. Februar ergänzen oder korrigieren würde.

Nach den Ereignissen in Österreich im Anschluß an die Zusammenkunft von Berchtesgaden trat die tschecho-slowakische Frage in den Vordergrund. Ich will Sie nicht im unklaren lassen, daß in Paris Leute aus verschiedenen Berufen und aus verschiedenem Milieu - davon Journalisten und Parlamentarier nicht ausgenommen - begonnen haben, ihrem Widerstand gegen den Gedanken, Frankreich müsse wegen der Tschecho-Slowakei mit Deutschland Krieg führen, Form und Ausdruck verleihen. Unter dem Einfluß der Denisches Flans wollten sowohl die Anhänger eines Abkommens mit Deutschland, als auch die Anhänger eines Abkommens mit Italien und schließlich die Gegner der Politik Frank-

Herrn Ph.Dr. Kamil K r o f t a ,
Minister des Auswärtigen,
P r a g .

Photostatic copy of first page of Document No. 4

I would only like to add that it would be important in regard to France and to other countries if Czechoslovakia were to have an independent standing in French policy. If the French Government were to make a statement in respect to Central Europe—Austria and the Little Entente— stating that it would fight on account of Central Europe, the impression would be created abroad that France was not seriously thinking of going to war, and, hence, for the sake of Czechoslovakia either, for it is obvious that France will not fight on behalf of every state in Central Europe. In France itself, a statement made in such a general form would only give a fillip to the policy propagated by Flandin and his like. If, after Berchtesgaden, and after the crisis in England, Delbos had only made a quite general declaration, the impression would have been created that France was renouncing her present policy. I was therefore fully aware that a firm declaration made specially in regard to Czechoslovakia, in distinction to a purely theoretical and general declaration on French policy in Central Europe, would not be of much use to Austria.[1] For me the chief thing was that, in respect to Czechoslovakia, there should be no doubt, all the more that from the very beginning we were up against the disinclination of the French to fight for the sake of Czechoslovakia. I will only briefly mention here an extremely important, and at the same time confidential, fact. On February 17, Delbos requested the British Government to define its position toward any further measures of pressure Germany might take against Austria, toward the Czechoslovak problem, and toward negotiations with Italy and Germany. Delbos wanted to have the answer before he made his speech in the Chamber. England was silent. On the evening of February 25, she sent her reply, which arrived in

---

[1] So in the original German translation.—*Ed*.

Paris on the morning of February 26, but did not reach Minister Delbos' hand before he made his speech in the Chamber at 11 o'clock. There can be no doubt that, in view of his depressed state of mind, it would have had a very bad influence on him. This influence would have been very harmful, because Delbos had rewritten his statement as far as it concerned Czechoslovakia several times, constantly reverting to a colourless and general declaration, until he finally settled on the declaration which I have already reported to you. It will certainly interest you to know that Delbos' statement on Czechoslovakia was greeted with approval by the entire Chamber. All the deputies applauded, except one: Pierre Étienne Flandin, who sat still without moving a muscle. At my request, supported by our friends at the Quai d'Orsay, Prime Minister Chautemps implicitly associated himself with Delbos' statement on Czechoslovakia.

The Senate Foreign Affairs Committee and Czechoslovakia

On February 23 a plenary meeting of the Senate Committee of National Defence (Army, Navy and Air) was held; it was presided over by Joseph Caillaux, Chairman of the Finance Committee, and was attended by Henry Bérenger, Chairman of the Foreign Affairs Committee. On February 25 (Friday), a meeting of the Foreign Affairs Committee took place, at which Chairman Bérenger made his report. He took advantage of the occasion to report his conversations with Minister Delbos on the results of the Berchtesgaden Conference and on the French démarche in London in respect to Austria and Czechoslovakia. Bérenger informed his colleagues that Minister Delbos and the Government had energetically demanded to know from England what she would do in the event that Berchtesgaden were to be repeated, and in the event that it were extended to Czechoslovakia. Chairman Bérenger stated that on Friday no reply had yet come from England. On Saturday, I lunched with Senator Bérenger, and he told me quite frankly that both in the Senate Foreign Affairs Committee and at the joint meeting of the National Defence Committee in respect to Czechoslovakia two questions were raised: had France a binding legal obligation toward Czechoslovakia, and 2)[1] was France in a position to come to Czechoslovakia's assistance. As regards the question of a binding legal obligation toward Czechoslovakia, Senator Bérenger told me that the thesis was advanced in his Committee that the Franco-Czechoslovak Treaty of Friendship had been an integral part of the Locarno Pact, and that since the Locarno Pact was no longer operative, the Franco-Czechoslovak Treaty was no longer binding. To this I replied that this argument was more than strange. When, shortly after the Locarno Treaty was concluded, Czechoslovakia sought to be allowed to participate in the Locarno consultations of the Great Powers and Belgium, the answer we received was that the Czechoslovak Treaty was not a component part of the Locarno agreement, and Czechoslovakia therefore was not entitled to take part in the consultations. Now it was being claimed that the Franco-Czechoslovak Treaty, as a component part of the defunct Locarno Pact, was also defunct. It was simply impossible to say the very opposite now to what was said to us for years after the Locarno agreement. Furthermore, the Franco-Czechoslovak Treaty of Friendship had an independent existence, since it was concluded in 1924, and even if Locarno no longer existed, which was a questionable assertion, the Franco-Czechoslovak Treaty of Friendship would nevertheless continue to exist as an independent treaty. Senator Bérenger said he was very grateful to me

---

[1] There is no figure "1" in the German.—*Ed.*

for this explanation, because they had been given an entirely different view of the matter. As to the second question, namely, whether France was bound and able to render Czechoslovakia military assistance, Senator Bérenger told me the theory had been advanced in their Committee that, because of the Maginot Line, France would be unable to come to Czechoslovakia's assistance, and that in order to do so, France would have to be in a position to march through Italy. I replied that formulated in this way the question was wrongly presented. The point at issue was not to explore the technical means by which France would come to Czechoslovakia's assistance, but whether France was prepared to declare war on Germany should she attack Czechoslovakia. Czechoslovakia was taking measures to be able to perform her duty, and she was prepared to perform it. If France did not wish to defend herself in Europe[1] in the event of an attack on Czechoslovakia, then naturally neither Czechoslovakia nor Central Europe could stand up against Germany. The mutual assistance which France and Czechoslovakia promised each other implied that if one of the contracting parties were attacked, the other would go to war against the aggressor. What assistance would be rendered technically besides this was a matter for the soldiers and for the future, for no one could say today where or how the war would be fought. Senator Bérenger replied that this viewpoint was new to him, and that he saw in it a possibility to achieve unanimity among the members of his Committee. Nevertheless, he considered it his duty to apprise me that besides the two questions mentioned and discussed by us there was the conviction of the members of the French Foreign Affairs Committee that France could do nothing in Central Europe without England. I replied that I knew that France and England

---

[1] So in the original German translation.—*Ed.*

der direkt oder indirekt angedeutet hätte, Frankreich solle seiner
Verpflichtung gegenüber der Tschecho-Slowakei nicht treu bleiben.

    Es grüßt Sie herzlich

           Ihr gez. Osuský .

F.d.R. gez.: Linh

Photostatic copy of last page of Document No. 4

depended on one another for self-defence. But while I knew that France needed England, I also knew that England needed France. I knew, for example, that if a question of the independence of Egypt were to arise, England would not say that she could and would do nothing for Egypt without the aid of France. England would simply take the necessary stand and would act in the conviction that France would have to assist her. Similarly, on the European continent, it was not England, but France that had vital interests, and it was to France and not England that the leadership and decision belonged. If France were to declare that a direct or veiled attack on Czechoslovakia would mean war with France, England would support France both diplomatically and politically, for it was to her interest that France should not be embroiled in war with Germany. This alone would be enough to avert war. Bérenger did not conceal that from the political and diplomatic standpoint my argument was quite correct.

On March 2 (Wednesday) Delbos made a report before the Senate Foreign Affairs Committee. The Franco-Czechoslovak Treaty of Friendship again came up for discussion. Ex-Premier Laval asked whether France was pledged in the event of an attack on Czechoslovakia to come to her assistance. Thereat Chairman Bérenger repeated the thesis he had expounded to me on February 26. In the matter of assisting Czechoslovakia, Chairman Bérenger said, the question for Czechoslovakia and France was whether they wanted to defend their independence or not. If they did, then, since they were mutually bound, they would declare war on an aggressor who attacked either one of them.

It is interesting that Delbos did not want it to be again mentioned in the Committee's communiqué that France remained faithful to her pledges; he only wanted it to be said that France would, in alliance with England, pursue a policy of national security and European peace. On Chairman Bérenger's insistence, the communiqué makes an express distinction between the continuation of close collaboration with England in the policy of national security and European peace, and the affirmation that the French Government will remain true to its commitments.

I would like to say that former President of the Republic and Member of the Senate Foreign Affairs Committee Millerand spoke very warmly and positively in favour of unreserved protection of Czechoslovakia. He said that France had never yet broken her pledged word, and that, moreover, it was in France's vital interest that there should be no doubt in anyone's mind that she will protect Czechoslovakia's independence by armed force. All through the long debate, not a single Senator hinted, either directly or indirectly, that France should not remain faithful to her obligations toward Czechoslovakia.

With cordial greetings, yours,

Osusky

No. 5

TELEPHONE CONVERSATION BETWEEN GOERING (BERLIN) AND RIBBENTROP (LONDON)

March 13, 1938, 9 h. 15 m.[1]

G: As you know the Fuehrer has entrusted me with the administration of the current government procedures [Fuehrung der Regierungsgeschaefte]. And therefore I wanted to inform you. There is overwhelming joy in Austria, that you can hear over the radio.

R: Yes, it is fantastic, isn't it?

G: Yes, the last march into the Rhineland is completely overshadowed. The Fuehrer was deeply moved, when he talked to me last night. You must remember it was the first time that he saw his homeland again. Now, I mainly want to talk about political things. Well, this story we had given an ultimatum, that is just foolish gossip. From the very beginning the National-Socialist ministers and the representatives of the people [Volksreferenten] have presented the ultimatum. Later on, more and more prominent people of the Movement

---

[1] Published in *Nazi Conspiracy and Aggression*, Office of United States Chief of Council for Prosecution of Axis Criminality, Washington, 1946, Vol. V, pp. 642-54 (Materials of the Nuremberg trial).—*Ed.*

Party participated, and as a natural result, the Austrian National-Socialist ministers asked us to back them up, so they would not be completely beaten up again and be subjected to terror and civil war. Then we told them we would not allow Schuschnigg to provoke a civil war, under no circumstances. Whether by Schuschnigg's direct order, or with consent, the Communists and the Reds had been armed, and were already making demonstrations, which were photographed with "Heil Moskau" and so on. Naturally, all these facts caused some danger for Wiener-Neustadt. Then you have to consider that Schuschnigg made his speeches, telling them the Fatherland Front [Vaterlandische Front] would fight to its last man, one could not know that they would capitulate like that and therefore Seyss-Inquart who already had taken over the government asked us to march in immediately. Before we had already marched up to the frontier since we could not know whether there would be a civil war or not. These are the actual facts which can be proved by documents. . . .[1]

G: But the Fuehrer thought because you are just there that you could inform the people what is really going on. Above all, that it is absolutely wrong to think Germany had given an ultimatum.

R: I have already spoken very openly with Halifax and Chamberlain. There is no doubt about it. Only the fact that the newspaper-people start to ask questions and it does not seem to be right if I still remain here, it would look strange, somehow.

G: No, no, I think so, too. Only, I did not know if you spoke already to these people. I want that you once

---

[1] Goering's assurances that universal enthusiasm reigned in Austria are omitted. For omissions, see *Nazi Conspiracy and Aggression*, Vol. V, pp. 643-46.—*Ed.*

more—but no—not at all once more—but generally speaking—tell the following to Halifax and Chamberlain: It is not correct that Germany has given any ultimatum. This is a lie by Schuschnigg, because the ultimatum was presented to him by Seyss-Inquart, Glaise-Horstenau, and Jury. Furthermore, it is not true that we have presented an ultimatum to the Federal President, but it also was given by the others and as far as I know just a military-attaché came along, asked by Seyss-Inquart, because of a technical question; he was supposed to ask whether in case Seyss-Inquart would ask for the support of German troops, Germany would grant this request. Furthermore I want to state that Seyss-Inquart asked us expressively—by phone as by telegram to send troops because he did not know about the situation in Wiener-Neustadt, Vienna, and so on; because arms had been distributed there. And then he could not know how the Fatherland Front might react since they always had had such a big mouth. . . .[1]

R: I had a long intensive conversation with Halifax, and I told him our basic conception also in respect to the German-English understanding—

G: That I wanted to say, you know yourself, Ribbentrop, that I always was in favour of a German-English understanding. No one else would be more glad than I, if the English really wanted it seriously, and if they also recognized that we are also a proud and free nation. After all, we also do represent 2 brother-nations.

R: I can tell you one thing, Mr. Goering. The other day I spoke to Chamberlain after that breakfast, and I got a very good impression of him, and he gave me a message,

---
[1] Part of the conversation relating to the internal situation is omitted. See *Nazi Conspiracy and Aggression*, Vol. V, pp. 646-47.—*Ed.*

some news for the Fuehrer, which I shall deliver personally to the Fuehrer. . . .[1]

R: . . . My conversations are concluded, and if I sit around it might give a funny impression. But I had an excellent impression of Chamberlain.

G: I am glad to hear that.

R: The other day I spoke quite a while with him. I do not want to speak about it over the phone, but I have the impression that Chamberlain also is very serious about an understanding. I told him in this conversation that after the Austrian problem had been settled, the understanding between Germany and England will be so much less complicated than before. I believe, he realized that.

G: Look, since the whole problem has been settled down there and no more danger of excitement and disturbance exists—and this was a source of real danger—the people should be thankful for our having eliminated this source of crisis.

R: I told them that, too, and also pointed out that we got rid of a situation, which caused always many troubles. Even if there was some excitement at this moment, the great line for the German-English understanding could only be strengthened by it. I also said to Halifax at the end of our conversation that we honestly do want to come to an understanding and he replied that his only worry was the CSR [Czechoslovakia].

G: No, no, that is out of the question.

R: I told him then that we were not interested and we did not intend to do anything there. On the contrary, if our Fellow-Germans were treated in a sensible way, then we should come to an agreement there, too.

---

[1] Part of the conversation relating to Ribbentrop's visit to Berlin is omitted. See *Nazi Conspiracy and Aggression*, Vol. V, p. 648.—*Ed.*

G: Yes, I am also convinced that Halifax is an absolutely reasonable man.

R: I got the best impression of Halifax as well as of Chamberlain. He thought it would be a little difficult with our (Engl.) public opinion, because there it looks like force etc. I have the feeling that the normal Englishman, the man in the street will say, why should England bother with Austria. . . . [1]

G: This is absolutely clear. (The following unintelligible.) [2] There are matters which do concern people, and there are matters which do not concern them at all.

R: I have to say through my last conversation with Halifax I have the impression that he did not react to the arguments I gave him, but at last he said I could be convinced that he also did favour a German-English understanding.

G: More or less everything is in wonderful peace. Two peoples embrace each other and are overjoyed and express their happiness. . . . [3]

---

[1] Part of the text is omitted because of its incoherence. See *Nazi Conspiracy and Aggression*, Vol. V, p. 649.—*Ed.*

[2] So in the American publication.—*Ed.*

[3] For the end of the conversation—on voting arrangements in Austria, Austrian diplomats, economic situation in Austria, etc,— See *Nazi Conspiracy and Aggression*, Vol. V, pp. 649-54.—*Ed.*

No. 6

TELEGRAM FROM THE GERMAN MINISTER IN PRAGUE EISENLOHR TO SECRETARY OF STATE IN THE GERMAN FOREIGN OFFICE WEIZSÄCKER[1]

Strictly Secret

TELEGRAM

Prague, March 18, 1938, 16 h. 55 m.
Received March 18, 1938, 18 h. 45 m.
   No. 60, 18.3
   To telegram of 17th, No. 40*)[2]
   *)[2] Department of Culture

For the Secretary of State

Promises of Henlein and Frank of March 15 communicated in telegram No. 57 of March 16. Both in separate conversations expressed their unreserved agreement. At Frank's wish a meeting has been appointed for next week with three representatives of the Sudeten Party to settle details of tactical action.

I did not in any way demand that the Sudeten Party should give up their oppositional stand or take up an active-

---

[1] Document from the Archives of the German Ministry of Foreign Affairs.

[2] So in the original.—*Ed.*

ly friendly attitude toward the State and the Government. On the contrary, I distinctly stressed that until it entered the Government after the elections the Party must remain in opposition, that it must not in its speeches express confidence in the promises of the *Government*,[1] but that it must inspire some hope in the population regarding German protection and in order to lessen the danger of incidents.

As the immediate aim, I indicated the realization of Hodža's assurances, with which they are there familiar, namely, the widest possible amnesty, the transfer of German officials and qualifying officials to the Sudeten German region, the development of self-government in such a manner that *later*[2] only German officials will be employed in the Government and self-government bodies; in addition, cessation of the building of schools for the spread of Czech influence,[3] the holding of government or municipal elections or both, and, further, the *participation of the Sudeten German Party in the Government*[4] with a view to acquiring wider rights and getting Czechoslovakia to withdraw from the pact system. Other cardinal aims mentioned were the abolition of the state police in the frontier region and the possibility of freely professing the National-Socialist weltanschauung. Conditions for entering the Government were not discussed, because they will not have any actual significance for months.

On the other hand, I put my foot down on the party organization's disposition to decline the permanent contact I had arranged with Hoff, and on the attempts to play off

---

[1] Underscored in the original.—*Ed*.
[2] Underscored in the original.—*Ed*.
[3] In the original: "Tschechisierungsschulen."—*Ed*.
[4] Underscored in the original.—*Ed*.

one against the other the different opinions and trends in foreign policy which are believed to exist in Germany, and to cast doubt on my authority as the official representative of Reich policy. Obstinate insistence on the present agitational demands of the Sudeten German Party, namely, on a Volksschutz law and "territorial autonomy," which are practically unfeasible and would be unacceptable to any *Czechoslovak Government*,[1] harbours the danger that in the end we shall either be forced to wash our hands of the Sudeten German Party, or we shall be drawn into an armed conflict.

Frank's verbal and written statements you have in your possession were made before his first talk with me on the evening of March 15, but in all essentials they correspond with the first talk. We must wait and see whether he now keeps his word.

Eisenlohr

---

[1] Underscored in the original.—*Ed.*

No. 7

NOTE FROM THE BRITISH FOREIGN OFFICE TO THE SOVIET EMBASSY IN LONDON[1]

No. C 1935/95/62

Copy
Foreign Office
24th March, 1938

Your Excellency,

[2] In continuation of my note of the 22nd March, I have the honour to inform Your Excellency that I have now read, and considered with great care, the text of M. Litvinov's statement to representatives of the press in Moscow, a translation of which you were so good as to communicate to me in your note of the 17th March.[3]

2. I note that this statement may be held to represent the point of view of the Soviet Government in regard to

---

[1] From the Archives of the Ministry of Foreign Affairs of the U.S.S.R.—*Ed.*

[2] The numeration of the first paragraph is not given in the original.—*Ed.*

[3] In its note of March 22, 1938, the British Foreign Office acknowledged the receipt of a note from the Soviet Plenipotentiary to the Foreign Office, dated March 17, 1938, inclosing the text of a statement made to press representatives by the People's Commissar of Foreign Affairs of the U.S.S.R. The statement was to the following effect:

"Having joined the League of Nations for the purpose of organized collaboration with the other peace-loving States, the Soviet Govern-

present international problems. I assume the substance of the Soviet Government's proposal to be that arrangements should be made immediately for a discussion to take place between the interested Governments with a view to determine the practical measures required in order to check the further development of aggression, and to counteract so far as possible the increasing danger of war.

3. His Majesty's Government would warmly welcome the assembly of an international conference, at which it

---

ment has never missed a suitable occasion to recommend the most effective guarantees of peace, which it has seen in the organization of the system of collective security within the framework of the League of Nations, as well as of a system of regional pacts of mutual assistance against aggressors. The Soviet Government adopted this way in practice when it concluded such pacts with France and Czechoslovakia, pacts which, in the absence of aggression, do not menace any State whatever. The violations of international undertakings ensuing from the League Covenant and from the Paris (Briand-Kellogg) Pact, and the attacks on some States by other States, which have occurred in the course of the past four years, have provided occasions for the Soviet Government to demonstrate not only its negative attitude towards these international crimes, but also its readiness to take an active part in all measures aiming to organize a collective rebuff to the aggressor, even disregarding the inevitable aggravation of its relations with the aggressor. At the same time, the Soviet Government voiced the warning that international inaction and the impunity of aggression in one case would inexorably lead to the repetition and multiplication of similar cases.

"Unfortunately, international developments have justified these warnings. They received a new confirmation in the armed invasion of Austria and in the forcible deprivation of the Austrian people of their political, economic, and cultural independence.

"While, formerly, outbreaks of aggression occurred in continents more or less remote from Europe or on the outskirts of Europe, and affected alongside with the interests of the victim of aggression the interests of only a few countries situated in the immediate proximity, this time the violence has been perpetrated in the centre of Europe and has created an indubitable menace not only for the eleven coun-

might be expected that all European states would consent to be represented, and where it might therefore be found possible to discuss in a friendly manner, and perhaps finally to settle, such matters as are thought most likely to endanger peace. In present circumstances, however, it would not appear that such a meeting could be arranged. A conference only attended by some of the European Powers, and designed less to secure the settlement of outstanding problems than to organise concerted action against aggression, would not

---

tries now contiguous with the aggressor, but also for all European States, and not only European ones. So far the menace has been created to the territorial integrity and, in any case, to the political, economic, and cultural independence of the small nations whose inevitable enslavement will, however, create the premises for pressure and even for attacks against large States as well.

"In the first place there arises the menace to Czechoslovakia, but owing to the contagious character of aggression, the danger threatens to grow later on into new international conflicts and already manifests itself in the alarming situation which has arisen on the Polish-Lithuanian frontier.

"The present international situation places before all peace-loving States, and the Great Powers in particular, the question of their responsibility for the destinies of the peoples of Europe, and not only Europe. The Soviet Government being cognizant of its share in this responsibility and being also cognizant of its obligations ensuing from the League Covenant, from the Briand-Kellogg Pact, and from the treaties of mutual assistance concluded with France and Czechoslovakia, I can state on its behalf that on its part it is ready as before to participate in collective actions, which would be decided upon jointly with it and which would aim at checking the further development of aggression and at eliminating the increased danger of a new world massacre. It is prepared immediately to take up in the League of Nations or outside of it the discussion with other Powers of the practical measures which the circumstances demand. It may be too late tomorrow, but today the time for it is not yet gone if all the States, and the Great Powers in particular, take a firm and unambiguous stand in regard to the problem of the collective salvation of peace."

necessarily, in the view of His Majesty's Government, have such a favourable effect upon the prospects of European peace.

4. In these circumstances, while sincerely grateful to the Soviet Government for having communicated to me their views upon the best course to be adopted to ensure the preservation of peace, I regret that His Majesty's Government cannot accept in their entirety the suggestions put forward by M. Litvinov in his statement under reference. The views of His Majesty's Government are being further elaborated in Parliament, and you will observe from the relevant statements of policy by His Majesty's Ministers that, though there may be a difference of opinion regarding the methods to be adopted, His Majesty's Government are no less anxious than the Soviet Government, to find effective means of strengthening the cause of peace.

I have the honour to be, with the highest consideration,

Your Excellency's obedient Servant,
[For the Secretary of State]

[signed] *C. W. Baxter*

No. 8

LETTER FROM COUNSELLOR IN THE GERMAN FOREIGN OFFICE ALTENBURG TO THE MINISTER IN PRAGUE EISENLOHR, ENCLOSING MINUTES OF A CONFERENCE ON THE SUDETEN GERMAN QUESTION, PRESIDED OVER BY RIBBENTROP[1]

Berlin, March 29, 1938

Pol. I 215 G
Secret [2]
Urgent

Minister Extraordinary and Plenipotentiary,
Herrn Eisenlohr (personally),

Prague

(By courier)

Referent: Legationsrat Altenburg

Herewith enclosed, strictly confidentially and for your personal knowledge, minutes of a conference on Sudeten German questions held today in the Foreign Office.

In accordance with the directives adopted at the conference, I request you to maintain, as heretofore, the closest

---

[1] Document from the Archives of the German Ministry of Foreign Affairs.

[2] Marginal note in pencil in Weizsäcker's hand: "Keep one copy of the enclosure for the Führer." The letter bears Ribbentrop's initial.—*Ed.*

possible contact with the Sudeten German Party, and, in your talks with Czechoslovak statesmen, to endeavour, although not officially, but as the opportunity offers, to support it in its forthcoming negotiations with the Czechoslovak Government in the manner agreed.

NOTES ON THE CONFERENCE ON 29 MARCH 1938, 12.00 HOURS, IN THE FOREIGN OFFICE ON SUDETEN GERMAN QUESTIONS[1]

In this conference the gentlemen enumerated in the enclosed list participated.

The Reichsminister (Ribbentrop) started out by emphasizing the necessity to keep the conference which had been scheduled strictly a secret; he then explained, in view of the directives which the Fuehrer himself had given to Konrad Henlein personally yesterday afternoon, that there were two questions which were of outstanding importance for the conduct of policy of the Sudeten German Party:

1. The Sudeten Germans must realize that they are backed up by a nation of 75 million which will not tolerate a continued suppression of the Sudeten Germans by the Czechoslovak Government.

It is the task of the Sudeten German Party to formulate such demands from the Czechoslovak Government as it deems necessary in order to obtain the privileges desired by it.

The Foreign Minister explained in this connection that it could not be the task of the Reich Government to give Konrad Henlein, whose position as the leader of the Sudet-

---

[1] Document from the Archives of the German Ministry of Foreign Affairs. This translation (together with Annex II) are taken from the American publication of the materials of the Nuremberg trial, *Nazi Conspiracy and Aggression*, Vol. V, pp. 422-24.—*Ed.*

en Germans has been expressly acknowledged and again confirmed by the Fuehrer, detailed suggestions about what to demand from the Czechoslovak Government. It is essential to propose a maximum program, which as its final aim grants full freedom to the Sudeten Germans. It appears dangerous to be satisfied prematurely with the consent of the Czechoslovakian Government; this on the one hand would give the impression abroad that a solution has been found, and on the other hand would only partially satisfy the Sudeten Germans. In any case, caution is the proper thing, because one cannot have any confidences in the assurances of Beneš and Hodža according to past experiences. The aim of the negotiations to be carried out by the Sudeten German Party with the Czechoslovakian Government is finally this: to avoid entry into the Government by the extension and gradual specification of the demands to be made. It must be emphasized clearly in the negotiations that the Sudeten German Party alone is the party to the negotiations with the Czechoslovakian Government, not the Reich cabinet [Reichsregierung]. The Reich cabinet itself must refuse to appear toward the Government in Prague or toward London and Paris as the advocate or peacemaker of the Sudeten German demands. It is a self-evident prerequisite that during the impending discussion with the Czechoslovak Government the Sudeten Germans would be firmly controlled by Konrad Henlein, would maintain quiet and discipline, and would avoid indiscretions. The assurances already given by Konrad Henlein in this connection were satisfactory.

Following these general explanations of the Reichminister the demands of the Sudeten German Party from the Czechoslovak Government as contained in the enclosure were discussed and approved in principle. For further cooperation, Konrad Henlein was instructed to keep in the closest possible touch with the Reichminister and the Head of the Central Office for Racial Germans [mit dem Leiter der Volksdeutschen Mittelstelle], as well as the German Minister in Prague, as the local representative of the Foreign Minister. The task of the German Minister in Prague would be to support the demands of the Sudeten German Party as reasonable, not officially, but in more private talks with the Czechoslovak politicians without exerting any direct influence on the extent of the demands of the Party.

In conclusion there was a discussion whether it would be useful if the Sudeten German Party would cooperate with other minorities in Czechoslovakia, especially with the Slovaks. The Foreign Minister decided that the Party should have the discretion to keep a loose contact with other minority groups if the adoption of a parallel course by them might appear appropriate.

Berlin, 29 March 1938

R[1]

---

[1] Ribbentrop's initial.—*Ed.*

ANNEX I

TO THE MINUTES OF THE CONFERENCE PRESIDED OVER BY RIBBENTROP

On March 29, 1938 [1]

I. *Immediate demands*: [2]

Aim: Pacification of the Sudeten Germans.

1. Municipal elections,
   political elections,
   elections to social institutions, (to switch the mood of the masses to positive action).
2. Broad amnesty.
3. Government order:

"Membership of the Sudeten German Party not to be made a reason for political persecution or for economic or social discrimination."

"Damage suffered in the past because of membership of the DNSAP or DNP to be immediately compensated."

II. Demands which must be satisfied *before* [3] the Sudeten German Party enters into concrete negotiations with the Government:

1. Retransfer of civil servants of German nationality from the Czech region and Slovakia to the German-inhabited region.

2. New appointments to civil service posts in the German inhabited region to be made only from among Germans.

New appointments to government offices and public institutions in areas with mixed populations and in central

---

[1] Document from the Archives of the German Ministry of Foreign Affairs.

[2] Underscored in the original.—*Ed*.

[3] Underscored in the original.—*Ed*.

departments to be made only from among Germans until conformity with the national composition of the population is attained.

3. Abolition of the state-police system and transfer of local police authority to the local government bodies (Gemeinden).

III. Demands which must be satisfied in the course of the negotiations between the Sudeten German Party and the Government:

1. The "Volk-Protection Bill" (Volksschutzgesetze), already introduced by the Sudeten German Party.

2. Revision of the parts of the Defence of the Realm Act which were from the very beginning directed against the Sudeten Germans.

3. Full restoration of local self-government.

4. German to have full rights as a state language.

5. Clarification of future foreign policy.

ANNEX II

TO THE MINUTES OF THE CONFERENCE PRESIDED OVER BY RIBBENTROP

On March 29, 1938

LIST OF THOSE PRESENT

In the Conference on Sudeten German Questions
On Tuesday, March 29, 1938, at 12 h. 00 m.

Present:

Reichsminister von Ribbentrop, State Secretary von Mackensen, Ministerial Director Weizsäcker, Ambassador Eisenlohr—Prague, Ambassador Stieve, Vortr. Legationsrat von Twardowski, Legationsrat Altenburg, Legationsrat Kordt	Foreign Office
SS Obergruppenführer Lorenz, Prof. Haushofer	Central Office for Racial Germans [1]
Konrad Henlein, Karl Hermann Frank, Dr. Künzel, Dr. Kreissl	Sudeten German Party

---

[1] In the original: "Volksdeutsche Mittelstelle."—*Ed.*

No. 9

LETTER FROM THE CZECHOSLOVAK MINISTER IN LONDON MASARYK TO CZECHOSLOVAK FOREIGN MINISTER KROFTA[1]

Ministry of Foreign Affairs *Secret*
Cabinet No. 1506 of Apr. 4, 1938 P o l. A r c h.[2]
Translation:
Czechoslovak Minister
9, Grosvenor Place S. W. 1,
London, April 5, 1938

Mr. Minister,

I have just had a long talk with Cadogan. I gave him a circumstantial and truthful account of the situation as I found it during my week's stay in Prague. He manifested a lively interest in every detail and it could be seen that the Foreign Office is deeply concerned in our affairs. I particularly stressed that the time had come when it was really essential that the British Government understood

---

[1] This document was seized by the Germans in the archives of the Czechoslovak Ministry of Foreign Affairs and translated by them from the Czech into German. The document in the possession of the Archives Department of the Ministry of Foreign Affairs of the U.S.S.R. is the German translation found in the files of the German Ministry of Foreign Affairs.—*Ed*.

[2] Stamp of the Political Archives of the German Ministry of Foreign Affairs.—*Ed*.

Ministerium für Auswärtige Angelegenheiten.
Kabinett Nr. 1506 vom 5.4.1938.

Geheim

Pol. Arch.

Übersetzung:

Czechoslovak Minister
9, Grosvenor Place S.W.1.
London, am 5. April 1938.

Herr Minister!

Eben hatte ich eine längere Unterredung mit C a d o -
g a n . Ich informierte ihn eingehendst und wahrheitsgemäss
über die Situation, die ich während meines einwöchigen Auf-
enthalts in Prag angetroffen hatte. Er zeigte ein lebhaftes
Interesse über alle möglichen Details und es war zu sehen,
dass unsere Angelegenheiten das Auswärtige Amt reichlich be-
schäftigen. Besonderen Nachdruck legte ich darauf, dass jetzt
die Zeit gekommen sei, wo es wirklich notwendig sei, dass die
englische Regierung begreife, dass aus den vermeintlichen Un-
terdrückern, für die wir hier gehalten wurden, Unterdrückte
geworden seien, dass wir das wilde Deutschland gegen uns hätten
und dass die entschlossene Disziplin, die unser Volk zeige,
bewunderungswürdig sei. Bei uns gebe es nicht nur 3 1/2 Million
Deutsche, sondern auch 10 Millionen Tschechen und Slowaken,
für die zum grossen Teil der ungebildete furor teutonicus
und die Notwendigkeit, auf sie Rücksicht zu nehmen, eine Belei-
digung und Erniedrigung sei. Ich machte auf das provokative
Benehmen der Henleinanhänger und auf die ganze engelshafte
Geduld des Ministeriums des Innern und der Regierung aufmerksam. Es scheint, dass meine Auslegung auf Cadogan Eindruck ge-
macht hat.

In der Unterredung gab Cadogan die offizielle Meinung
in folgenden Punkten kund:

1) Die Regierung und das Auswärtige Amt erachten es von
unserer Seite für opportun, mit Henlein und nicht nur mit
seinen Parteileuten zu sprechen. Ich entgegnete, dass Dr. Hodža eine Unterredung mit Henlein vorbereite.

2) Er bat, dass sie über Newton und über mich informiert

Photostatic copy of first page of Document No. 9

that, from the supposed oppressors we were here taken to be, we had become the oppressed, that we had a wild Germany against us, and that the firm self-control displayed by our people was worthy of admiration. We had not only three and a half million Germans in our country, but also ten million Czechs and Slovaks, for the greater part of whom the savage furor teutonicus and the necessity of having to reckon with it is an insult and humiliation. I drew attention to the provocative conduct of Henlein's followers and to the truly angelic patience of the Ministry of the Interior and the Government. It seemed that Cadogan was impressed by my account.

In the course of the conversation Cadogan set forth the official opinion in the following points:

1) The Government and the Foreign Office consider that it would be opportune on our part to begin negotiations with Henlein, and not only with members of his party. I replied that Dr. Hodža was preparing for a talk with Henlein.

2) He requested that they should be kept informed through Newton and myself of what was going on and what was being contemplated, and agreed that too much haste should not be shown, since the matters in question were of such fundamental importance.

3) France had no government and Paul-Boncour was not a Foreign Minister who at so serious a moment could be a worthy partner in a discussion of the European crisis.

4) There was deep distrust of Russia and doubt whether she could effectively intervene outside her borders. This did not mean that Russia could not be utilized politically; on the contrary, it was in Czechoslovakia's interest to keep the danger of Russian intervention before the eyes of the Germans, because, notwithstanding all assurances, Germany was afraid of Russia.

5) Cadogan promised that they would work in Berlin for reconciliation, by pointing out there that the negotiations should not be broken off, for otherwise the achievements would not be worth much.

6) He had sufficiently convincing information that heavy industry in the German regions did not want to be joined to Germany at any price, and that the Austrian aristocracy, who were largely our aristocracy, were now in a position similar to that of the Jews, and that they stood for our State.

I took this opportunity to say that it was precisely the aristocracy that had always most shamefully blackened our State, and that their ambassador in Berlin received all information unfavourable to us from this source. Cadogan smilingly agreed (Cadogan is a real aristocrat, dignified but modest, Nevile Henderson is a big snob,[1] and our Mr. Newton a petty snob).

Cadogan assured me of his good will and intimated in Halifax's name that, although he could not give me any binding promise, should we as occasion arose need their help, they would do everything within the bounds of possibility.

Yours very respectfully,

Signed: *Jan Masaryk*

Dr. Kamil Krofta
Minister of Foreign Affairs,
Prague

---

[1] In the original: "bedeutender Snob."—*Ed.*

würden,was geschehe und sich vorbereite und er gab zu,dass
man sich nicht allzu sehr beeilen könne,da es sich um eine
Angelegenheit von so grundlegender Wichtigkeit handle.

3) Frankreich hat keine Regierung und Paul Boncour
ist nicht der Aussenminister,der in einer so ernsten Zeit
ein würdiger Partner bei einer Verhandlung über die europäische Krise sein würde.

4) Grosses Misstrauen gegenüber Russland und Zweifel
darüber,dass es ausserhalb seiner Grenzen tatkräftig ein-
greifen könne.Das bedeutet aber nicht,dass sich politisch
mit Russland nicht operieren lasse,im Gegenteil,liege es
im Interesse der Tschechoslowakei,den Deutschen die Ge-
fahr eines russischen Eingreifens vor Augen zu stellen,weil
trotz aller Versicherungen Deutschland vor Russland Angst
hat.

5) Cadogan versprach,dass sie in Berlin für eine Ver-
söhnung arbeiten werden,indem sie darauf hinweisen,dass
die Verhandlungen nicht abgebrochen werden sollen,da sonst
die Erfolge nicht viel wert sein würden.

6) Er hat genügend eingehende Nachrichten,dass die
Schwerindustrie in den deutschen Gebieten um keinen Preis
zu Deutschland will und dass sich die österreichische,d.i.
zu einem grossen Teile unsere Aristokratie,jetzt in einer
ähnlichen Situation wie die Juden befindet und dass sie
positiv zu unserem Staate steht.

Ich habe die Gelegenheit benützt,um ihm zu sagen,
dass es gerade die Aristokratie war,die immer auf die
schändlichste Art unseren Staat angeschwärzt hat und dass
ihr Botschafter in Berlin alle für uns ungünstigen Infor-
mationen aus diesen Quellen hat.Cadogan stimmte lächelnd
zu (Cadogan ist ein wirklicher Aristokrat,bescheiden selbst-
bewusst,Neville Henderson ist ein bedeutender Snob und
unser Herr Newton ein kleiner Snob.)

Cadogan versicherte den guten Willen und dass er mir
im Namen Halifax´s die Versicherung gebe,dass sie,wenn wir
von Fall zu Fall ihre Hilfe brauchen würden,obwohl er mir
keine bindenden Versprechungen geben könne,alles tun werden,was in den Grenzen der Möglichkeit sein wird.

Es empfiehlt sich Ihnen in Ehrerbietung

gez. Jan M a s a r y k .

Herrn Dr.Kamil K r o f t a
Minister für Auswärtige Angelegenheiten
in P r a g .

No. 10

STATEMENT BY MR. CHAMBERLAIN AT A MEETING OF BRITISH AND FRENCH MINISTERS[1]

MR. CHAMBERLAIN'S REPLY TO M. DALADIER

April 28, 1938

The Prime Minister asked M. Daladier to believe that he had listened to the statement of the French Premier with emotion. His blood boiled when he saw Germany extending her domination over Europe and registering success after success. But it was necessary to remember the interests at stake. If one contemplated speculating in this matter, then it was a speculation not with money but with human beings. This thought was undoubtedly present in M. Daladier's mind as it was in his, Neville Chamberlain's mind. It was impossible to calculate the disasters to France and England which would result from a conflict, and it was doubtful whether the two countries were strong enough to impose their will upon Germany, even at the price of suffering and terrible losses. For his part, the Prime Minister did not think France and England were at present strong enough for this; he agreed with what M. Daladier had said yesterday about the growing defensive power, and the time might come

---

[1] Quoted by Georges Bonnet, in his *Defense de la Paix. De Washington au Quai d'Orsay* (pp. 352-53), from the record of the London conference of British and French Ministers.—*Ed.*

when it would be possible to resist under better conditions. But at the present moment the British public would not consent to accept such a responsibility, and it would not be wise for the Government to go beyond what the public can accept.

Mr. Neville Chamberlain furthermore wondered whether the European situation was as black as M. Daladier believed. He doubted very much that M. Hitler desired the destruction of the Czechoslovak State, or of a refashioned Czechoslovak State; he did not believe the Führer wanted an Anschluss. It was doubtless for that reason that M. Henlein had not mentioned it, despite the sentiments of his followers. It went without saying that the desire was simply suspended, and would be reverted to later; however, it ought to be possible for M. Beneš to make proposals which, while altering the character of the Czechoslovak State, would prevent its destruction. If Germany wanted its destruction, then the Prime Minister quite frankly could not see how she was to be prevented; but he did not believe that this was wished in Berlin. . . .[1]

. . . It was evidently impossible to exclude the possibility of war entirely, since things more precious than life or property might be at issue; but it should be embarked on only as a last resort, and not lightheartedly. The Prime Minister had witnessed a war, and had seen how impossible it is for anyone to emerge from it stronger or happier. It was therefore only under the dictate of the most pressing necessity that one could resign oneself to it. Mr. Neville Chamberlain declared that he emphatically rejected all thought of a preventive war.

---

[1] Ellipsis in the original.—*Ed*.

No. 11

REPORT OF THE POLISH AMBASSADOR IN PARIS LUKASIEWICZ OF A CONVERSATION WITH THE FRENCH FOREIGN MINISTER BONNET[1]

EMBASSY OF THE POLISH
REPUBLIC IN PARIS   Copy

No. 1/F/18
Re: Conversation with Foreign Minister
Bonnet

POLITICAL REPORT No. XVII/2
Strictly Confidential
Paris, May 27, 1938

The Minister of Foreign Affairs,
    Warsaw

Today, at 11 h. 45 m., I called upon Minister Bonnet in accordance with your instructions of the 24th inst., No. 8, Berlin.

Desiring to be as exact as possible, I read to M. Bonnet a practically word for word translation of the text received from you. M. Bonnet wrote down my statement, considering it to be a communication of prime importance.

After reading my statement twice, M. Bonnet, as on the occasion of our previous conversation, did not proceed at once to discuss it, but began with general remarks. He told

---

[1] Original in Polish.

me that he had had a talk with General Gamelin on the subject of our strategical position in the event that Czechoslovakia were occupied by the Germans, and that the French General Staff considered that this would greatly and very dangerously prejudice our military position. Bonnet intends to continue his talks with representatives of the French Army on this subject in order to study the arguments in greater detail. However, he requested that I at once draw the attention of my Government to the above. Next, M. Bonnet expressed the conviction that although the German-Czech conflict had arisen over the question of the German minority, yet when analyzing this conflict it was necessary to look beyond the minority problem and to realize that the issue at stake was the maintenance of peace and the checking of Germany's dangerous expansion in Central Europe. "There are many national minority problems," my vis-à-vis remarked. "Today we are occupied with some, in the future we shall be occupied with others." This was an indirect, but in my opinion not malicious, hint at our national minority problems.

Then, proceeding to discuss my communication, M. Bonnet said that the French Government was not asking anything of Poland in connection with the Czechoslovak problem, but the French Government would like to be able to reckon on our co-operation in the maintenance of peace, as well as in counteracting German expansion. If the Polish Government did not consider it possible to present a declaration to Berlin analogous to that of the British Government, it might publish a declaration which would not contain any new commitments but would announce that the Polish Government deemed it necessary to take every measure for the maintenance of peace, that certain events might lead to a general conflict, and that, lastly, Poland could not remain impassive in such a situation and still did not

O d p i s.

Ambasada R.P. w Paryżu

Nr.1/E/18.

W sprawie: rozmowy z p.Min. Bonnet.

RAPORT POLITYCZNY Nr.XVII/2

ŚCIŚLE-TAJNE.

Paryż, dnia /maja 1938 r.

Ambasada Rzeczypospolitej Polskiej
Berlin

PANA MINISTRA
SPRAW ZAGRANICZNYCH
W W A R S Z A W I E.

W dniu dzisiejszym o godz.11 m.45 udałem się do Ministra Bonnet, celem wykonania instrukcji Pana Ministra z dn. 24.V. b.r. Nr.8 Berlin.

Pragnąc być jaknajbardziej ścisłym, odczytałem Ministrowi Bonnet prawie dosłowne tłomaczenie tekstu, który otrzymałem od Pana Ministra, min.Bonnet cały mój komunikat zanotował, uważając, iż jest on oświadczeniem pierwszorzędnej wagi. Po dwukrotnym odczytaniu mego komunikatu min.Bonnet, jak w poprzedniej rozmowie nie odrazu przystąpił do omówienia go, lecz zaczął od uwag natury ogólnej. Powiedział mi mianowicie, iż rozmawiał z gen.Gamelin na temat naszej sytuacji strategicznej w wypadku, gdyby Czechosłowacja była zajęta przez Niemcy i że sztab francuski uważa, że byłoby to ogromnym i bardzo niebezpiecznym pogorszeniem naszej sytuacji wojskowej. Ma zamiar kontynuować rozmowy z przedstawicielami armii francuskiej na ten temat, aby poznać szczegółowiej argumenty, prosi jednak, abym już teraz zwrócił uwagę mego rządu na powyższe.

Otrzymuje:

Ambasada R.P. - Londyn -
Ambasada R.P. - Berlin -

Photostatic copy of first page of Document No. 11

know which of the belligerent sides she would have to join. Bonnet requests you to consider the possibility of our publishing such or a similar declaration, and to let him know.

Then M. Bonnet began to speak at length, and with manifest emphasis on this problem, of relations with the Soviet Union in the present situation and, to a certain extent, divorced from it. The Franco-Soviet pact, he said, was very "vague"[1] and the French Government was not at all inclined to rely upon it. It would play a role and be of importance only in connection with the way Poland's vacillations were taken in France. M. Bonnet personally was no adherent of collaboration with Communism. The French Government wanted to rely entirely on Poland and to cooperate with her. It would like our relations as allies to be more precisely defined and extended. M. Bonnet would be very pleased if, after elucidating the question of collaborating with Poland, he could tell the Soviets that France does not need their assistance.

However, the positive sides of the Franco-Soviet pact should not be overlooked. In the event of war with Germany the pact would serve as a basis for demanding of Moscow such assistance in the form of materiel and raw materials as might be needed. In certain circumstances Poland might utilize the pact to her advantage.

Under present conditions it might be affirmed that the Franco-Soviet pact would not have to play an important role, if the Franco-Polish alliance could become fully effective.

Having thus elucidated the problem of Soviet Russia, M. Bonnet passed to the question of our minority in Czechoslovakia. Here he manifested not only uneasiness, but even

---

[1] In the original Polish text this word is written in French, and in inverted commas.—*Ed*.

a certain irritability. I shall try to convey what he said in the following lines:

The question of the Polish minority in Czechoslovakia was not analogous to that of the German minority, both because of the size of the population involved in the two cases, and because the Polish minority concerned a State which was bound by alliance with France. Moreover, this minority resided in the territory of a State with which France was friendly. It might be said with confidence that after the question of the German minority had been settled, Czechoslovakia would have to proceed to settle the question of the Polish and other minorities. However, it would be highly vexatious and inexplicable if, as a result of acting on your views, Mr. Minister, Poland's demands respecting the minority were to complicate the situation and cause new tension, and, as might be expected, at exactly the moment the Sudeten question was being adjusted. The French Government appreciated the importance of the minority question to Poland, but the Polish Government must not make use of this question for actions that might lead to still more serious complications or prevent the Polish Government from adopting a favourable attitude toward the Anglo-French efforts for a peaceful settlement of the conflict that might arise between Germany and Czechoslovakia. It was highly unpleasant and dangerous that you, Mr. Minister, not only declined to undertake the démarche in Berlin in which the French Government is so interested and to define Poland's attitude in the event of a Franco-German conflict, but on top of this were putting forward new demands, and moreover in so immoderate a form as to be fraught with new difficulties and dangers.

Seeing that M. Bonnet was not acquainted with the matter, or did not understand the communication I had made in your name, or did not want to understand it (which is less likely), I interrupted him and said that not a single new demand was being advanced by us in this instance.

The question of our minority in Czechoslovakia was of long standing, and all this time the Prague Government had done nothing to settle it, except make promises. Nor had the sympathy and influence of the French Government been of any effect in the course of many years. In no circumstance could we tolerate for a moment that the problem of the Polish minority be settled after the settlement of the question of the Sudeten Germans. This problem must be settled simultaneously and on entirely analogous lines with the settlement of the problem of the Germans. Size of population was of no consequence or importance. For that matter, if I was not mistaken, the Czechoslovak Minister in Warsaw had informed the Polish Foreign Minister about a fortnight ago that the Czech Government recognized our right to the most favoured nation clause with respect to the Polish national minority, in other words, was willing to grant the Polish minority the same rights as may be granted to the German minority. I could not understand why the communication of the Polish Foreign Minister on this subject, made with the object of informing the French Government of our position and attitude, as well as of the significance of the problem, should arouse such uneasiness and agitation. Surely, M. Bonnet did not think we could or would wait for the settlement of the question of our minority until the problem of the Sudeten Germans had been successfully settled, as I hoped it would be. With the settlement of the Sudeten German problem the present tension would end; the influence of the Powers in Prague would become what it was before the conflict, and Czechoslovakia would return to her old policy of not fulfilling her promises. This would be too naive, and

Polish public opinion would not understand such a policy, and would not stand for it. I thought that if M. Bonnet turned his attention to this problem and carefully analyzed it, he would realize the correctness and necessity of the stand we were taking.

After this rejoinder of mine, M. Bonnet considerably moderated his tone, and somewhat modified his attitude toward the problem. He did not revert to the thesis of a separate settlement of the problem of our minority, and in the further course of the conversation he took care to impress upon me that we should not attach too much political importance to this question, that in the end it would be settled, and that the French Government would see to it that it was settled. In the course of his argument, Bonnet said that he would like us to state the rights we sought for our minority more specifically. I replied that as a matter of fact, in order to avoid unnecessary complications, and taking into account that our minority was smaller than other minorities, all we asked was that our minority should be regarded as having equal rights with other, larger minorities. Having thus parried M. Bonnet's arguments on the subject of the minority, I said that I would report to you all his remarks and questions and would await further instructions. Meanwhile, I said, I would like to communicate to him some of my personal observations.

As regards General Gamelin's opinion that our strategical position would be greatly and dangerously prejudiced if Germany seized the whole of Czechoslovakia, although I was not a military man, I believed he was perfectly right. Only I could not understand why attention was drawn to this, since in my opinion the assumption was purely theoretical and was absolutely precluded. I did not know whether Hitler wanted autonomy for the Sudeten Germans or the annexation of the territory they inhabited. But I had never heard that he was out for the annexation of the whole of Czechoslovakia. I therefore considered that reflections on the situation, which General Gamelin probably assessed correctly, were pointless. As regards the possibility of our undertaking a démarche in Berlin with the object of easing the situation, which M. Bonnet had suggested, I considered that we had already done exactly what he wished. We had done so, not in the form of a démarche in Berlin, but in connection with the report in the *Evening Standard*, when, in our denial, we publicly declared that in the event of serious complications we reserved the right to make our decisions. I emphasized that this ought to be considered a valuable contribution on our part to the efforts for the maintenance of peace.

Lastly, I added, in order to avoid misunderstanding or unclarity, I ought to point out that in the talks between General Gamelin and Marshal Rydz-Smigly the question of material assistance and aid in the form of raw materials from Soviet Russia was raised by General Gamelin, but that Marshal Rydz-Smigly categorically excluded talk or discussion on this subject; there was therefore nothing to refer to. I did not say a word on the subject of Soviet Russia, bearing in mind that your instructions were not to discuss it, and knowing that in the present situation the subject was inappropriate. To these brief remarks of mine, M. Bonnet replied that perhaps the presumption that Germany would annex all Czechoslovakia was too hypothetical, but that Goering's plan to partition Czechoslovakia between Germany and Hungary and to turn over Teschen Silesia to Poland was no secret. The effectuation of this plan would be equivalent to the annexation of the whole of Czechoslovakia, and the annexation of the territories inhabited by the German minority would greatly worsen Poland's position from the military standpoint.

I replied that in my opinion it was absolutely unthinkable to presume that in the twentieth century, after a great war, a result of which was the triumph of the national principle, any State, even one stronger than Germany, could annex territories inhabited by other nations against their will. I expressed the belief that if the Czechs were determined to fight for the Sudetenland, they would certainly defend Prague to the last drop of their blood. I acknowledged the correctness of the view that if the present conflict were to end with the annexation of the Sudetenland by Germany, this would worsen the strategical position of Czechoslovakia.

Taking advantage of my reference to the talks between Marshal Rydz-Smigly and General Gamelin regarding possible assistance from Soviet Russia, M. Bonnet reverted to the question of the Franco-Soviet pact and said the following:

Should a conflict arise between Poland and Germany, the Franco-Soviet pact might be of positive value to Poland, first, by eliminating the likelihood of a fight on two fronts, and, second, by affording the possibility of assistance in the form of materiel and raw materials. That a conflict between Germany and Poland was probable could not be doubted. Stresemann, in his time, had categorically affirmed in private conversation with M. Bonnet that Germany would never agree to the existing frontier with Poland. It was hard to believe that this view in Germany had cardinally changed since the National-Socialists came to power. Consequently, an improvement of relations with Russia would undoubtedly be of value to Poland.

M. Bonnet then again reverted to the question of the minority, and stressed that we should not draw too far-reaching conclusions with respect to so important a problem as the maintenance of peace in Europe. In his opinion, we should pay attention to public opinion in France. The denial published after the report in the *Evening Standard* had made a most painful impression on the French public. French public opinion was deeply disappointed by Poland's attitude, and it would undoubtedly be profoundly shocked if it learned that Poland not only refused to undertake a démarche in Berlin and to define her position in the event of a Franco-German war, but was preparing to make things even worse by couching her demands in a very trenchant form. It was necessary to be cautious. It would be very desirable if the Polish Government could find an appropriate way in which to confirm that it was taking part in the efforts for a peaceful settlement of the conflict, and that it set great value on them.

My reply was roughly as follows:

I was surprised that our denial produced such a painful impression on French public opinion; I presumed that this was also the way it was received in Berlin. In my opinion, our denial should be regarded as a valuable contribution to the cause of peace. I was glad that M. Bonnet had referred to public opinion, as I wished to draw his attention to the necessity of caution in this respect, as well as to the necessity of concern being displayed on the part of the Quai d'Orsay respecting the behaviour of the French press. I remarked that there was still alive among the Polish public the unpleasant memory of the unfriendly attitude of the entire French press toward us at a time when Poland was experiencing great difficulty in connection with the Lithuanian incident. We remembered the deplorable (néfaste) conduct of French diplomacy in the settlement of a problem of such vital importance to Poland. The impression was still alive in our memories that at that crucial moment for Poland not only was France not on our side, but, on the contrary, she, ignoring our interests, was absorbed with the question of the possible passage of Soviet troops through the territories of other countries in the event of a war with Germany. In such circumstances, any fresh attacks on the part of the French press would be more than undesirable.

At this point of the conversation, M. Bonnet tried to assure me that France after all did advise Lithuania to make her peace with us, to which I replied that I had no wish to start a discussion on this point, because it would be too painful, and I would like to have the opportunity to forget it. Then, in an amicable but categorical form, I declared that our most important duty at this moment was to further the efforts toward mutual understanding of the interests and positions of our States. We were situated at two different ends of Europe, and therefore we might have different interests and different views, but we were allies. Poland was situated in a part of Europe where a policy was being pursued without consideration for our interests, and often against them. This policy was one of the reasons for the present situation, and that too should be taken into consideration.

I believed that the French Government would duly appreciate the Polish Foreign Minister's declaration of readiness to discuss all problems involved in the developing situation.

To this statement of mine M. Bonnet reacted very animatedly and even, I would say, cordially, and declared that the French Government desired to establish the closest contact with us, that it set high value on such contact, and that he would like to see me more often so as to have the opportunity to discuss every phase of the swiftly developing events. I replied that I would always be at his service, and that as soon as I had anything useful to impart I would come on my own initiative. This ended our conversation, which lasted 1 h. 15 m. and was of a friendly character, in spite of certain ticklish moments.

I ought to add that in the course of the conversation M. Bonnet said that France had the support not only of England, but also of the United States. I presume he had in mind the statement of Under Secretary of State Sumner Welles published in today's dispatches, which the French press interprets as proof that the sympathies of the Americans are on the side of France, Britain and Czechoslovakia.

I am quite certain that until yesterday evening nothing else had come from Washington. Ambassador Bullitt told me that M. Bonnett had said in a talk with him that he did not entertain the thought that the United States might support the British and French démarche in Berlin, to which Ambassador Bullitt replied that he was definitely right. This confirms how little M. Bonnet needs to assert that a particular State is on the side of France.

Ambassador of the Polish Republic

No. 12

REPORT OF THE GERMAN AMBASSADOR IN LONDON VON DIRKSEN TO THE MINISTRY OF FOREIGN AFFAIRS[1]

Secret

POLITICAL REPORT[2]

London, July 10, 1938
FO, Berlin

Supplementary to Report
A. No. 2589, of June 10, 1938

Re: Present State of German-English Relations

I. There has scarcely been another instance in the history of Anglo-German relations when they have in so short a time been so thoroughly discussed—I would almost say: upset—in their totality as in the past three months. The political relations were put to a severe test by the Austrian Anschluss and the Czechoslovak crisis; the problem of Austria's debts raised the question of the economic and financial relations of the two countries; England's denunciation of the passport agreement threatened passenger traffic and, hence, the possibility of a proper rapprochement; the

---
[1] Document from the Archives of the German Ministry of Foreign Affairs.

[2] The original bears an inscription in red pencil: "From Ambassador von Dirksen. 18.8."—*Ed.*

London, den 10. Juli 1938.

A.A.Berlin

Im Anschluss an den Bericht
A.2509 vom 15. Juni d.Js.

) Doppel
(1 " f.Pol.Abt.)
(1 " f.d.Dn.Botsch.)

G e h e i m !

Politischer Bericht.

Inhalt: Der gegenwärtige Stand der
deutsch-engl. Beziehungen.

I.

Kaum jemals in der Geschichte der
deutsch-englischen Beziehungen ist die Gesamtheit dieser Beziehungen innerhalb so kurzer
Zeit so grundlegend zur Diskussion gestellt
man möchte fast sagen: erschüttert worden,
wie das während der vergangenen drei Monate
der Fall gewesen ist. Die politischen Beziehungen wurden durch den Anschluss Österreichs und die tschechoslowakische Krise einer
Belastungsprobe unterworfen; die Frage der
Übernahme der österreichischen Schulden rol
die Wirtschafts- und Finanzbeziehungen beider
Länder auf, die Kündigung des Paß-Abkommens
durch England bedrohte den Reiseverkehr und
damit....

Photostatic copy of first page of Document No. 12

British Government's military and economic war preparations—especially the organization of air defence—raised in the minds of the population the spectre of an impending war; the reincorporation of Austria and the "Niemöller affair" reawakened half-forgotten agitational complexes, such as the Jewish question and the Church question. The foundations on which Anglo-German relations were erected tottered; they were threatened by blows from without—for the first time since the end of the world war, it was not a German-French, but a German-English conflict (it goes without saying, with the participation of France, Czechoslovakia, etc.) which came under the lurid limelight of the world press. These peace-menacing developments took their course notwithstanding the fact that Germany, even on the admission of her enemies, had not committed any act that might constitute a threat to peace, and notwithstanding the fact that in England the Chamberlain-Halifax Cabinet is at the helm and the first and most essential plank of its platform was and is agreement with the totalitarian States.

Hence it is an urgent necessity to analyze the causes that have called forth these developments and to find the means of eliminating this menacing state of affairs.

II. The chief reasons for the developments which are driving toward a crisis in German-English relations are, in my opinion, the following:

1) *The three driving forces that are anxious to unleash a war by a world coalition against Germany* [1] in order to destroy her before she has fully established her position as a World Power—Jewry, the Communist International and the nationalist groups in the individual countries—have not for a long time been so persistently and feverishly active as in these past months. After a series of vain attempts to unleash a world war—such as the bombing of the cruiser

[1] Underscored in the original.—*Ed*.

Leipzig, the spread of sensational rumours regarding German intentions in Morocco, the attempt of the second Blum Cabinet in March of this year to employ French regular divisions in Spain—these same forces renewed the attempt to set a world coalition against Germany by staging the Czech week-end crisis. This action was prepared, accompanied and, after the failure of the conspiracy, continued by a campaign in the press, for which the revival of the Jewish question in Austria and the Church conflict in Germany were to furnish the fuel.

2) These sinister machinations found fertile soil in British public opinion all the more since the *Austrian Anschluss*[1] had shocked the political conscience of the Britons. The old catchwords about the right of existence of small nations, democracy, the League of Nations, the mailed fist of militarism were revived, and profoundly agitated and disturbed the average Englishman who readily responds to every appeal to his sentimentality. Of far greater importance still was the fact that the politically-minded Englishman imagined that he had been tactically outwitted and that his power on the continent was threatened. Together with the purely human reaction, "not to be fooled again," the political determination was strengthened to oppose, even at the cost of war, any further attempts to change the balance of power on the continent without a preliminary understanding with England. This determination was for the first time openly expressed during the Czech crisis.

3) To this general attitude of English public opinion was added the state of mind which, in a democratic country, is inseparably associated with rearmament. If opposition was to be removed, the credits for armament obtained, and the necessary number of volunteers for the army and

---

[1] Underscored in the original.—*Ed*.

air defence secured, the people had to be roused. To achieve this, it was not enough to persuade the public that there was a theoretical danger of war; it had to be demonstrated that there was a threat from a concrete enemy. All these considerations and tendencies resulted in the creation of an atmosphere which engendered a neurotic fear of a possible attack by a possible enemy. And this possible enemy could only be Germany.

4) These developments were accelerated by the fact that the *whole complex of German-English relations was being more and more drawn into the vortex of British domestic politics*.[1] By making his major aim the achievement of an adjustment with the authoritarian States independently of the League of Nations, and using this cry to get rid of Eden, Chamberlain—after the conclusion of the Italo-English treaty—gave his opponents the opportunity to select the German-English adjustment, or, rather, its impossibility, as the chief and nearest target for attack. For the non-eventuation of this adjustment would reduce Chamberlain's major thesis to an absurdity. Consequently, the attacks of the British press on the alleged rape of Austria and on Germany's intention to annex Czechia at the same time brought grist to the mill of Chamberlain's foes.

These foes chose German-English relations as a target for direct and indirect attack also from the following considerations of domestic political tactics: the parliamentary opposition—the Labour Party and the Liberals—as a result of a rather complicated evolution, were led to select as the ground for their attacks, not domestic, but foreign policy. Here Germany was an object all ready at hand on which they could vent their hatred of authoritarian state leadership. The same, if for quite different reasons, is true of Chamberlain's enemies within his own party:

---
[1] Underscored in the original.—*Ed.*

Eden and the Churchill group. Eden and his followers, because they believe that the authoritarian States can be curbed only by direct threat of war, are following the leading strings of the parliamentary opposition. Churchill, together with his followers, believes that the easiest way to overthrow Chamberlain and put himself in the saddle is to accuse the Cabinet of dilatoriness in building sound defences against possible attack—on the part of Germany, of course. It goes without saying that it is presumed that this attack will come from the air—regarding the threat of which the average Englishman is just now as sensitive as he was regarding the "German Luxusflotte" before the war. Chamberlain had therefore to save himself from the attacks of the opposition by kicking out his Air Ministers, Winterton and Swinton; hence, too, the attack of Member of Parliament Sandys in connection with the insufficiency of anti-aircraft guns. The effect of all these manoeuvres, which for the most part are prompted by purely domestic political considerations, is that the average Englishman pictures Germany as the probable enemy, and one who will perhaps have to be fought soon.

The result of this internal and external development of German-English relations is that the relations between the two countries are in a state of complete uncertainty. The attempts to effect an adjustment made in the talks held from the autumn of 1937 to 1938 were interrupted owing to Chamberlain's declaration on March 23 of this year in connection with the Austrian Anschluss. Of the two pillars on which, even in critical times, the shaky edifice of foreign relations rested—the economic treaty and the naval limitation agreement—the economic treaty was shaken by the question of Austria's debts; the new agreement, however, was made effective, and it has had a favourable indirect general influence. The naval agreement is liable to alteration owing to the development of the naval armament policy of the Great Powers; its political value has been undermined by the consciousness that has been spreading in England in the past few years, and especially in the past few months, that the most dangerous threat to England's security is now, not the navy of an eventual enemy, but the air force. No long arguments are needed to demonstrate that a general regulation of German-English relations must be striven for, if developments fraught with a serious danger of war are to be averted.

III. The premises for the possibility of a general settlement of the problems which divide the two countries are indicated in the following questions:

1) Have the developments of these past months diminished or destroyed the readiness of the Chamberlain Cabinet to seek an adjustment with Germany?

2) Is the Chamberlain Cabinet strong enough to carry through a policy of adjustment?

In reference to the first question. The shock of the Austrian Anschluss caused the reaction with which we are familiar, but it was comparatively quickly overcome. The blunders of British foreign policy during the Czech week-end crisis were soon recognized as such, and steps were taken to remedy them by acknowledging the loyalty demonstrated by Germany, by remaining silent in face of the vigorous attacks of the German press, by a speech by Halifax friendly to Germany in the House of Lords, by his speech before the Royal Institute of International Affairs containing a broad recognition of the German standpoint, by Chamberlain's speech in Kettering, and by Halifax's statements to the press on July 11.[1]

All these pronouncements on the part of responsible British statesmen, which were emphasized and interpreted

---
[1] So in the original.—*Ed.*

in conversations with me, are evidence that the desire for agreement with Germany stands—with a growing tendency, however, to let Germany take the initiative for the resumption of the negotiations. In point of time, this readiness coincides with a certain clarification of the Czechoslovak question.

There is a wish in London to remove this question, as a breeding ground of a new world war, from the immediate field of danger, if only through a temporary and tentative agreement between the Sudeten Germans and the Czechoslovak Government, before entering on so far-reaching a new political undertaking as an attempt at an adjustment with Germany.

In reference to the second question. The Chamberlain Cabinet has in these past months been the object of a growingly fierce attack on the part of its opponents, without its having any correspondingly conspicuous achievements to show. The only big achievement, the settlement with Ireland, is totally ignored. The Anglo-Italian treaty has not yet entered into force, since the stipulations relative to the developments in Spain have not been carried out. The acceptance of the combing plan[1] likewise cannot be represented as an achievement, since its execution is dubious and at the best will take several months. Relations with Germany, which is being increasingly suspected and abused by the opposition and the press, have been subjected to strain, so that still less could there be any question of adjustment. Chamberlain's foreign policy program of agreement with the totalitarian States has in no case been fully successful—at best it has promissory notes of dubious negotiability to its credit. On the other hand, the Cabinet has sustained painful wounds from the attacks of the oppo-

---
[1] The plan to eliminate foreign volunteers from the Republican army and so-called "volunteers" from Franco's army.—*Ed.*

sition: Air Ministers Winterton and Swinton had to be thrown overboard in order to absolve the Cabinet of the charge of displaying insufficient energy in air armament; the Sandys-Hore Belisha conflict over the violation of military secrecy, or parliamentary privileges, is at present at best a draw; Chamberlain's statements regarding England's agricultural potentialities and limitations have incurred the rancour of the British farmers, who represent the core of the Conservative vote. However, in spite of all these attacks, it is unlikely that the Cabinet will be in serious danger before the summer recess. The vacation months, if there are no dangerous developments in foreign policy, will have an assuaging effect. The confidence in Chamberlain's personal integrity and firmness prevalent in wide sections of the electorate will be reinforced by the recognition that there is no other man in the opposition equal to him. The desire to reach an adjustment with Germany exists among the broad mass of the British people and is popular.

After a few months of more tranquil developments Chamberlain and Halifax will have the determination, and the assurance from the standpoint of domestic politics, to tackle the last and most important task of British policy: an adjustment with Germany.

IV. To sum up, it may be said:

1) German-English relations, in their totality, are uncertain and extremely strained. They are in need of adjustment—or at least of an attempt at adjustment—if it is to be avoided that, as was the case before 1914, the conviction gain ground with the British Government (present or future) that the defeat of Germany by a world coalition is essential for the security of the British Empire.

2) The present British Cabinet is the first post-war Cabinet which has made agreement with Germany one of

the major points of its program; therefore this government displays with regard to Germany the maximum understanding that could be displayed by any of the likely combinations of British politicians. It possesses the innerpolitical strength to carry out this task. It has come nearer to understanding the most essential points of the major demands advanced by Germany, with respect to excluding the Soviet Union from the decision of the destinies of Europe, the League of Nations likewise, and the advisability of bilateral negotiations and treaties. It is displaying increasing understanding of Germany's demands in the Sudeten German question. It would be prepared to make great sacrifices to meet Germany's other just demands—on the *one* [1] condition that it is endeavoured to achieve these ends by peaceful means. If Germany should resort to military means to achieve these ends, England would without the slightest doubt go to war on the side of France. The military preparations are sufficiently advanced for this; so are the war-economic preparations; the mental preparation of the English people for such an eventuality, as the last few months have shown, has been completed; the political trial mobilization during the Czech crisis showed that the foreign political deployment [2] has been effected on a scale at least as great as the world coalition of 1914.

3) The attempt to effect an adjustment with England will therefore be the most urgent task of our foreign policy, as soon as suitable conditions will have been created for it in the course of the next few months.

Signed: *von Dirksen*

---

[1] Underscored in the original.—*Ed.*
[2] In the original: "aussenpolitischer Aufmarsch."—*Ed.*

3.) Der Versuch, einen Ausgleich mit England herbeizuführen, wird daher die vordringliche Aufgabe unserer Aussenpolitik sein, sobald die nächsten Monate die stimmungsmäßigen Voraussetzungen dafür geschaffen haben werden.

        gez. von Dirksen.

Photostatic copy of last page of Document No. 12

No. 13

CHURCHILL'S MEMORANDUM OF HIS CONVERSATION WITH THE HEAD OF THE DANZIG FASCISTS FOERSTER[1]

MEMORANDUM OF MR. CHURCHILL'S INTERVIEW
WITH HERR FOERSTER,

On July 14, 1938 [2]

After the usual preliminaries, I [3] said I was glad the anti-Jewish laws had not been introduced in Danzig. Herr Foerster said the Jewish problem was not acute in Danzig, but he endeavoured to learn whether that kind of legislation in Germany was an obstacle to an understanding with Britain. I replied that it was harmful and irritating, but that it was probably not an absolute obstacle to a working agreement because the reasons for it were understandable. He seemed to attach great importance to this point and reverted to it in the subsequent course of the conversation.

Herr Foerster asked whether I had ever been in his part of the country, and suggested that I pay it a visit.

---

[1] The original from which this translation was made is a German translation of the English text made in the German Ministry of Foreign Affairs in 1943. It bears the notation: "Translation from the English."—*Ed.*

[2] Caption to the German translation.—*Ed.*

[3] I. e., Churchill.—*Ed.*

I replied that if I went to Poland, I would stop over at Danzig. He then pressed me to go to Poland through Germany, in order to meet Hitler. I said that a conversation between an almighty dictator and a private person was scarcely likely to be useful, and asked whether August and September would not be unhealthy[1] months for a visit to Germany. He replied that no one in Germany was thinking of war, that they had vast social and cultural plans which it would take years to realize, that the Party congress would take place in September, and that there could be no question of incidents or serious complications then. When we reverted to this point later, Herr Noé, his interpreter, said that the situation was similar to that of 1914, when no one in Germany thought of war but everyone in England feared it, to which I replied that unfortunately we were right.

Herr Foerster asked what possible reasons could there be for war, whereupon I mentioned the situation in Czechoslovakia. Some solution could surely be found for it, and I told him that I had the feeling after my talks with Henlein and Masaryk that this should be possible even within the framework of the Czechoslovak State. I assured him that Britain and France would make every effort to persuade the Prague Government to give their consent, but he said that the influence of Moscow had induced them again to take up a stiff and impudent attitude. He asked what would happen if the Czechs refused to follow the advice of Britain and France, to which I replied that I was certain they would.[2] He said rather pointedly that he hoped it would be soon.

I remarked that I did not believe that Germany really feared Russia, to which he replied that they knew for a

---

[1] In the original: "ungesunde."—*Ed.*
[2] So in the original.—*Ed.*

fact of the existence of Russian airfields in Czechoslovakia, from which an attack could be launched on Berlin in half an hour. I replied that, in my opinion, it would be quite possible, as part of a general European agreement to pledge Britain and France to come to Germany's assistance with all their forces should she be the victim of an unprovoked attack on the part of Russia through Czechoslovakia, or in any other way. He asked who was to determine who was the aggressor. I replied that the aggressor would be the nation that first forcibly crossed the frontier of another nation.

I said that it rested with Herr Hitler to earn eternal renown for himself and to do an immense service to Germany and the whole world by relieving us of the oppressive fear of war. He said that Herr Hitler had repeatedly offered to disarm, if other nations did likewise, that they had tried one-sided disarmament unsuccessfully, and that Germany could not remain a second-rate nation when she was in danger of attack from heavily armed neighbours. I said we could at any rate endeavour to reach agreement regarding the rules of air warfare, to which he replied that Hitler had made the proposal to abolish bombers, but had received no reply; if the matter was to be raised again, it was for England to take the first step.

I said that I was no opponent of German might, and that most people in England would like to see her take her place as one of the two or three leading world Powers; that we would not resent the peaceful and gradual growth of German commercial influence in the Danube Basin, but that any violent action would almost inevitably lead to a world war. The situation was steadily deteriorating. All countries were squandering their means on armament. We had even built factories in Canada so that we might have an unlimited supply of aircraft in the third or fourth year of war. It lay with Hitler to dispel the clouds. We would help.

Herr Foerster said he saw no real grounds for a conflict between Britain and Germany; if Britain and Germany could only come to terms, they could divide the world between them. (The interpreter thought it better not to translate this last remark.)

The visit concluded with a repeated invitation to visit Hitler, and the inquiry whether I could come if I received an invitation; to this I gave a non-committal answer.

No. 14

LETTER FROM UNDER SECRETARY OF STATE IN THE GERMAN FOREIGN OFFICE WOERMANN TO THE GERMAN LEGATIONS IN BUCHAREST AND BELGRADE[1]

Berlin, July 25, 1938

S e c r e t [2]

1. German Legation in Bucharest
2. German Legation in Belgrade

We have learned confidentially of an incident which occurred several weeks ago bearing on Rumania's attitude toward the passage of Soviet troops through Rumanian territory.

According to this information, the French Foreign Minister—in order to stress as strongly as possible the difficulty of Czechoslovakia's political situation—told the Czechoslovak Minister in Paris that M. Comnen had informed him personally that Rumania would never tolerate the passage of Soviet troops through her territory. M. Bonnet is said to have added that Rumania had made a declara-

---

[1] Document from the Archives of the German Ministry of Foreign Affairs.

[2] Notation in red pencil: "By urgent courier"; and in ink: "Courier 25/7."—*Ed.*

tion to this effect in Berlin and Warsaw. Thereupon the Czechoslovak Foreign Minister telegraphed M. Comnen saying he understood Rumania's attitude in this matter, but was surprised that he had found it necessary to make such a declaration in Berlin. In his reply, M. Comnen denied he had made such a declaration in Berlin. He said that no one could demand that Rumania should consent in advance to the passage of Soviet troops. Rumania knew on which side she would stand in the event of war. This explanation is said to have satisfied M. Krofta.

We have been further confidentially informed that the Yugoslav Premier intends, during the meeting of the Council of the Little Entente in Bled, to advise M. Comnen to make a statement to Germany on the subject of the possible passage of Soviet troops through Rumania.

I request you after acquainting yourself with this letter to destroy it.

By order,
(Under Secretary of State)
W.[1]

---

[1] Woermann's initial.—*Ed*.

Berlin, den 25. Juli 1938.

Geheime Reichssache u.St.S.

An

1. die Deutsche Gesandtschaft in Bukarest
2. die Deutsche Gesandtschaft in Belgrad

Geheim!

Aus vertraulicher Quelle haben wir von einem einige Wochen zurückliegenden Vorgang Kenntnis erhalten, der sich auf die rumänische Haltung in der Frage des Durchmarsches von Sowjettruppen durch rumänisches Gebiet bezieht.

Danach soll der französische Außenminister - um möglichst stark die Schwierigkeiten der politischen Lage der Tschechoslowakei hervorzuheben - dem tschechoslowakischen Gesandten in Paris gesagt haben, Herr Comnen habe ihm persönlich erklärt, daß Rumänien niemals einen Durchmarsch der Sowjettruppen durch sein Gebiet dulden werde. Herr Bonnet scheint hinzugefügt zu haben, Rumänien habe eine Erklärung dieser Art in Berlin und in Warschau abgegeben. Daraufhin soll der tschechoslowakische Außenminister an Herrn Comnen gedrahtet haben, er verstehe die Haltung Rumäniens in dieser Frage, wundere sich aber, daß

Photostatic copy of first page of Document No. 14

daß er eine solche Erklärung in Berlin
habe abgeben müssen. In seiner Antwort
soll Herr Comnen bestritten haben, in
Berlin eine derartige Erklärung abgegeben
zu haben. Er habe gesagt, niemand könne
von Rumänien verlangen, daß es im voraus
in einen Durchmarsch der Sowjettruppen
einwillige. Rumänien wisse, wo es im
Falle eines Krieges stehen würde. Diese
Erklärung soll Herrn Krofta befriedigt
haben.

Wie wir weiter vertraulich erfahren,
soll der jugoslawische Ministerpräsident
in Aussicht genommen haben, Herrn Comnen
gelegentlich der Tagung des Rates der
Kleinen Entente in Bled in der Frage
eines etwaigen Durchmarsches von Sowjettruppen durch Rumänien anzuraten, eine
Erklärung an Deutschland abzugeben.

Ich bitte diesen Erlaß nach Kenntnis-
nahme zu vernichten.

Im Auftrag
(U.St.S.)

Photostatic copy of last page of Document No. 14

No. 15

REPORT OF THE POLISH AMBASSADOR IN BERLIN LIPSKI TO FOREIGN MINISTER BECK[1]

EMBASSY OF THE POLISH
REPUBLIC
No. N1/137/38

M. Jozef Beck,
Minister of Foreign Affairs

Berlin, August 11, 1938
Strictly Confidential

Highly esteemed Mr. Minister,

Since I had the honour on the 5th inst., during your passage through Berlin, to give you a verbal account of Sudeten developments as seen from here, I have received information which throws additional light on the matter.

Of interest is the opinion of the British Ambassador, who displays great independence of judgment. The other day he told one of my colleagues that in his opinion Premier Chamberlain had taken upon himself a great responsibility in sending Lord Runciman to Prague. The Ambassador particularly stressed that Runciman's mission was taken very seriously on the English side, and that the purpose was not to achieve a temporary and superficial solution, but a fundamental settlement of the matter. Should Lord

---

[1] Original in Polish.

Runciman, in spite of all his efforts, fail to secure agreement, it would then be clear, if the blame for the failure lay with the Czechs, that the Germans were right when they asserted that owing to the intransigence of the Czechs the only effective means was force.

The Ambassador intimated that in that event the British Government would renounce all further responsibility. I also know that Sir Nevile has used his influence with the Rumanian and Yugoslav Ministers with a view to getting their Governments to exert pressure on Prague. He did this, he said, on his own responsibility, without instructions from his Government. According to later information, both Bucharest and Belgrade were to intervene in Prague to induce the Czech Government to make concessions.

Further, I had the opportunity to talk with American Ambassador Wilson after his return from Warsaw and Prague. As he has known Beneš for some considerable time, ever since he was Minister in Switzerland, the President of the Czech Republic invited him for a talk. Ambassador Wilson told me that, unlike the past, when Beneš was very sure of himself, today he resembles a man who is under strong stress and is seeking a way out.

Beneš denied that the main resistance to the Sudeten demands came from him, and stressed his peaceful intentions. While indicating that he was prepared to consent to the granting of local self-government on the basis of national curiae, he declared he could not agree to the Sudeten demand for territorial self-government.

In answer to my question, Wilson also said that Beneš would not agree to recognize the Sudeten Germans as a people with their own state.[1] The American Ambassador was further surprised to find that, while the authorities

---

[1] In the original: "Staatsvolk."—*Ed.*

Ambasada Rzeczypospolitej Polskiej

Berlin, dnia 11 sierpnia 1938 r.

Nr. N/1/137/38

Ściśle tajne.

do P.Józefa Becka
Min.Spraw Zagran.

Wielce Szanowny Panie Ministrze,

Od czasu, kiedy miałem zaszczyt w dniu 5 b.m. przedstawić ustnie Panu Ministrowi w czasie przejazdu Jego przez Berlin rozwój sytuacji sudeckiej, widziany z tutejszego terenu, uzyskałem szereg informacyj, rzucających dalsze światło na sprawę.

Ciekawą jest opinia Ambasadora Angielskiego, który w swych sądach wykazuje dużą niezależność. Wypowiedział on się w tych dniach wobec jednego z moich kolegów w tym sensie, iż uważa, że Premier Chamberlain wziął na siebie bardzo dużą odpowiedzialność, wysyłając Lorda Runcimana do Pragi. Ambasador podkreślił z naciskiem, że misja Runcimana jest traktowana jak najbardziej poważnie ze strony angielskiej i że nie chodzi tu o krótkotrwałą powierzchną solucję, lecz o zasadnicze załatwienie sprawy. Gdyby Lord Runciman mimo swych wysiłków nie doprowadził do porozumienia, to wówczas stałoby się jasnym, jeśli wina niepowodzenia leżałaby po stronie czeskiej, że strona niemiecka ma słuszność, twierdząc, że wobec nieustępliwości Czechów jedynie droga siły jest skuteczna.

Photostatic copy first page of Document No. 15

in Prague were alive to the seriousness of the situation, the broad mass of the people underrated the danger.

Toward the end of the conversation Mr. Wilson remarked, with the reservation that this was only his personal opinion, that he had the impression that in selecting Lord Runciman, who belongs to the Liberal Party, Chamberlain was guided by consideration for the internal political situation in England, and perhaps also in France.

At yesterday's reception at the Italian Ambassador's in honour of Marshal Balbo, I had the opportunity to exchange views with Field-Marshal Goering. Goering said that he would like in the very near future to have a longer talk with me and to discuss—of course, confidentially and unofficially, as usual—the possibility of closer Polish-German contact on certain matters. By way of example he mentioned the mutual cessation of espionage activities and, further, a certain exchange of information on the Russian and Czech problems.

In reference to the Russian problem, he said in a general way that it would acquire actuality after the settlement of the Czech question. He reverted to his idea that in the event of a Soviet-Polish conflict Germany could not remain neutral and refrain from rendering assistance to Poland. He denied the rumour that Germany wanted to march against the Ukraine, and emphasized that the Reich's interest was concentrated primarily on putting an end to Bolshevik activities. On the other hand, Poland, in his opinion, might have certain direct interests in Russia, for example, in the Ukraine.

At this point of the conversation I informed Goering of the conversation between Vice-Minister Szembek and Comnen, in the course of which the latter had categorically expressed his opposition to the passage of Soviet forces through Rumanian territory. Goering was pleased to hear this.

When I asked him about the Sudeten question, Goering intimated that the matter was drawing to a close ("Die Sache geht jetzt zu Ende"). He believed that the Czech State would cease to exist, as a creation patched together of the most diverse nationalities: Germans, Slovaks, Hungarians, Ruthenians, and, lastly—a certain number of Czechs. Goering casually mentioned that the moment was approaching when a decision would have to be taken and agreement reached on this problem. In Goering's opinion, the Western Powers were beginning to realize that the present situation was intolerable. England had undertaken mediation, as he put it, more as a formality. The Czechs were chiefly relying on the relations of Prague with the Soviets.

In the course of these remarks Goering said—and this I consider very significant—that *in the event of a conflict over the Sudeten question the Italians surely could not allow the Reich to be attacked by France.*[1]

In view of the situation that has arisen in connection with Lord Runciman's mediation, Regent Horthy's forthcoming visit to Germany, and also the above-mentioned statements of Goering to the effect that the Sudeten question was nearing a climax, I deemed it appropriate to go a step further than what had hitherto been said in my conversations with Goering. I stressed that already at the time of the Paris Conference it had been the policy of the Czechs to have a common frontier with the Soviets, and to inordinately extend their territory along our southern border. This deprived us of a direct frontier with Hungary, which was contrary to Polish-Hungarian interests, which rest upon age-old traditions of the two States. *Goering replied that he realized the necessity for a common Polish-Hungarian frontier.*[2]

---

[1] Underscored in the original.—*Ed.*
[2] Underscored in the original.—*Ed.*

The subsequent exchange of views with Goering touched only on a few questions concerning our direct relations, such as our seasonal workers, whose labour capacity the Field-Marshal values very highly, and whose number he would like to increase next year. We also touched on the happy conclusion of the Polish-German economic negotiations, and on the social insurance agreement.

At this same reception I had a brief talk with the Hungarian Minister. Touching on Regent Horthy's visit to the Reich, I said, in accordance with your instructions, that I would feel honoured to have the opportunity to pay my respects to the Regent during his stay in Berlin. Minister Sztojay was pleased to hear this and said that Horthy would most likely receive me on August 24.

In the further course of the conversation I stressed how important the present moment was for our mutual relations, and added that Warsaw and Budapest were in constant contact. Remarking that I was speaking in a private capacity, I expressed misgiving that in the discussion of the Sudeten question Hungarian and Polish interests in Czechoslovakia might be neglected. The Minister seemed to share this opinion.

I further remarked that I regarded Runciman's mission rather sceptically, because Prague would refuse to accept the major demands regarding the Sudetens. I added, however, that, on the other hand, I could not yet detect any clearly defined German line. I therefore believed that it would be in our interest to take whatever timely measures were necessary. Minister Sztojay agreed with this. He strongly stressed Hungary's need of Poland's support. Nevertheless, he betrayed a note of uncertainty, for example, when he expressed misgivings as to Yugoslavia's attitude and Rumania's resistance to a possible Soviet demand to permit the passage of troops.

On the basis of the above-mentioned conversations, which I shall take the liberty to supplement with authoritative statements after a lengthier conversation with Goering, one gets the following picture:

The German Government does not believe in the success of the Runciman mission, and the more radical elements, among whom I include Field-Marshal Goering, believe that this question cannot be settled without resort to force. Should Beneš really reject the demands respecting the "Staatsvolk" and territorial autonomy, the possibility of achieving agreement seems more than doubtful, unless England confronts Czechoslovakia with the alternative: either accept the German demands, or England will withdraw and leave Czechoslovakia to face the Reich alone. We have therefore to reckon with the possibility of a crisis. Chancellor Hitler, as I have again heard from several reliable sources, declares for the benefit of the outside world that he will not go to war over the Sudeten. This position of the Chancellor's, incidentally, accords with the state of mind of the broad German public—with the exception of the fanatical sections of the Party and the youth—which are disturbed by the possibility of international war complications. I receive information to this effect from all parts of the country.

The older generation is undoubtedly influenced by the memory that the Great War was lost in spite of the excellent state of preparation in 1914. At the same time, however, feverish activity is being developed to safeguard the Reich in the event of a conflict with the West, which finds expression in the building of fortifications with a maximum strain of materials and manpower.

I should here like to draw attention to the contacts between Italian and German military circles, which have of late become very intense; I shall only mention the last

— 6 —

Francji przez Włochy w razie konfliktu niemiecko-czeskiego na temat Sudetów pozwalam sobie zwrócić tutaj uwagę na dość charakterystyczny ustęp mowy Marszałka Balbo, wygłoszonej w odpowiedzi na przemówienie Göringa w dniu 10 b.m. :

> "Niemcy i Włochy pozostaną niezwyciężone, jeśli prowadzoną przez Mussoliniego i Hitlera swoją politykę wspólnie realizować będą"

> /"Deutschland und Italien werden unbesiegbar bleiben, wenn sie, geführt von Benito Mussolini und Adolf Hitler, ihre Politik gemeinsam verfolgen"/.

Raczy Wielce Szanowny Pan Minister

przyjąć wyrazy mego wysokiego poważania i szacunku

J. Lipski

Photostatic copy of last page of Document No. 15

visit of the Italian Chief of Staff Pariani and the present visit of Marshal Balbo. In addition to the above-mentioned view of Goering, that Italy would check France in the event of a German-Czech conflict over the Sudetens, I take the liberty of drawing your attention to a rather significant passage in the speech made by Marshal Balbo in reply to Goering's address on the 10th of this month:

"Germany and Italy will be invincible if, led by Benito Mussolini and Adolf Hitler, they pursue their policy in common."[1]

Accept, etc.

J. Lipski

---

[1] In the original, the passage in inverted commas is repeated in German.—*Ed.*

No. 16

MINUTE OF A CONVERSATION BETWEEN ASHTON-GWATKIN, COUNSELLOR TO THE BRITISH FOREIGN OFFICE AND THE LEADER OF THE NAZI SUDETEN GERMAN PARTY HENLEIN[1]

Copy
Secret

CONVERSATION BETWEEN K. H.[2] AND ASHTON-GWATKIN IN THE PRESENCE OF PRINCE HOHENLOHE, ON AUGUST 22, 1938, FROM 14 h. 30 m. TO 16 h. 30 m., IN THE CARLTON HOTEL, MARIENBAD

A. began with a few courteous remarks to K. H. The day before he had been at the Reichenberg Fair and at Bad Liebwerda. They had been very cordially greeted by the population and had had another opportunity to see how devoted the people were to K. H. It had already been said on the Czech side that Mr. Runciman was too strongly influenced by K. H. R. and his colleagues were certainly very favourably impressed by the Sudeten Germans.

---

[1] Document from the Archives of the German Ministry of Foreign Affairs.

[2] The abbreviations of names in the original are retained in the translation: K. H.—Konrad Henlein; A.—Ashton-Gwatkin; B.—Beneš; R.—Runciman.—*Ed*.

Abschrift.

Geheime Reichssache!

Geheim

Gespräch K.H. mit A s h t o n - G w a t k i n im Beisein von
Prinz H o h e n l o h e am 22.8.1938 in der Zeit von 14,30 -
16,30 Uhr im Carlton-Hotel zu Marienbad:

- -

Einleitend sagt A. K.H. einige Höflichkeiten. Er wäre
tags zuvor bei der Reichenberger Messe und in Bad Liebwerda gewesen. Sie seien von der Bevölkerung sehr herzlich begrüsst worden
und sie konnten sich wieder überzeugen, wie die Bevölkerung an
K.H. hänge. Von tschechischer Seite sei bereits geäussert worden,
dass Herr R u n c i m a n sich zu stark von K.H. beeinflussen
lasse. R. und seine Mitarbeiter hätten allerdings von den Sudetendeutschen den besten Eindruck.

Die Unterhaltung bewegte sich zunächst in der Erörterung von Teilproblemen, wobei K.H. nochmals auf seine Anschauung
über die Möglichkeiten einer Lösung der sudetendeutschen Frage zu
sprechen kam:

1.) die Lösung, die die Tschechen bisher anstrebten, d.h.
Vernichtung des Sudetendeutschtums,

2.) Gewährung einer vollen Autonomie,

3.) Volksabstimmung und Abtretung.

Man kam auf die Notwendigkeit sofortiger Massnahmen zur
Schaffung einer besseren Atmosphäre zu sprechen. K.H. sähe diese
Möglichkeit nur, wenn die Regierung etwa folgende Erlasse durchführt:

1.) Sofortige Zurückziehung der tschechischen Staatspolizei
und Wiedereinführung der Gemeindepolizei,

2.) Strenges Verbot der Verfolgung Sudetendeutscher wegen
ihres Volkstums und ihrer politischen Betätigung,

3.) Strenge Bestrafung von Übergriffen von Beamten, Militär
und Polizei,

4.) Verbot jeglicher Hetzpresse und Grenzlerhetze,

5.) Sofortiger Beginn der Versetzung deutscher Beamter ins
deutsche Gebiet,

6.) Sofortige Aufhebung der unerträglichen Zensurpraxis.

A. fragt, ob R., der in den nächsten Tagen bei B e -
n e s c h sei, anfragen soll, welche konkreten Vorschläge er vor
habe. (Die Engländer hatten inzwischen von dem bekannten Vorschlag B. über Univ.Prof. S a n d e r erfahren).

K.H.: Es wäre jedenfalls interessant, dies zu erfahren.

A. äussert, dass es Ihnen am angenehmsten wäre, wenn B
selbst mit einem tragbaren Vorschlag käme.

Photostatic copy of first page of Document No. 16

The conversation then gravitated around individual problems, during which K. H. again expounded his views on the possible solutions of the Sudeten German question:

1. The solution the Czechs have been striving for until now, namely, the destruction of the German character of the Sudetenland.

2. Granting of complete autonomy.

3. Plebiscite and cession.

The conversation turned on the necessity of taking immediate measures to create a better atmosphere. K. H. thought this was only possible if the government issued approximately the following orders:

1. Immediate withdrawal of the Czech state police and restoration of the communal police.

2. Strict prohibition of persecution of Sudeten Germans on account of their nationality or political activity.

3. Severe punishment of abuses on the part of officials, the military or the police.

4. Prohibition of all incitation in the press and hounding of the border population.[1]

5. The taking of immediate steps to transfer German officials to the German region.

6. Immediate abolition of the intolerable censorship.

A. asked whether R., who was to see Beneš within the next few days, should ask him what concrete proposals he had in mind. The English had by this time learned of the proposal made by B. through University Professor Sander.[2]

K. H.: It would at any rate be interesting to know them.

A. said that it would please them most if B. himself made an acceptable proposal.

K. H. again pointed out that not only was the Sudeten German problem involved, but German-Czechoslovak re-

---

[1] In the original: "Grenzlerhetze."—*Ed*.

[2] In the original: "über Univ. Prof. Sander erfahren."—*Ed*.

lations as well. He again illustrated at length the manifestations of incorrigible Czech enmity toward the Germans, and the pressure the Czechs were exercising on the Sudeten Germans who remained true to their nation. There was not the least sign that the Czechs contemplated changing their course.

A. asked whether, if the Czechs in the coming week betrayed no intention of coming to terms, K. H. was prepared *to sound out the Führer as to the desirability of a meeting even before the Party Congress* [1] between British representatives and the Führer, at which not only the Czechoslovak question might be discussed.

K. H. asked what other possible points of discussion he had in mind.

A.: He could not say definitely, but he supposed an *air pact, the colonial question, and an armament agreement.* [2]

K. H.: He would be travelling all the next week and could not go to Germany before the week was over. Moreover, such a step could be contemplated only if it were the wish of the British Government.

A.: He would let him know about it, since he intended going to London in the next few days.

On August 23, in the evening, after a conversation Runciman had with Beneš, A. rang up Hohenlohe and requested him to arrange a meeting between Runciman, himself and K. H. on Sunday, August 28, at the Rotenhaus.

On August 24 A. left by air for London.

Mutual promises of an early meeting were made at the parting.

---

[1] Underscored in the original.—*Ed*.
[2] Underscored in the original.—*Ed*.

Geheim!

K.H. verweist nochmals darauf, dass es sich nicht nur um das sudetendeutsche Problem handle, sondern um das Verhältnis Deutschland-Tschechoslowakei. Er illustriert nochmals eingehend die Äusserungen der unbelehrbaren Deutschfeindlichkeit seitens der Tschechen und den Druck, den das Tschechentum gegen das volkstreue Sudetendeutschtum ausübe. Es seien nicht die geringsten Anzeichen dafür vorhanden, dass die Tschechen sich eines Besseren besönnen.

A. fragt, wenn in der kommenden Woche die Tschechen kein sichtbares Entgegenkommen zeigen, ob dann K.H. bereit wäre, beim F ü h r e r zu sondieren, ob noch vor dem Parteitag eine Aussprache zwischen englischen Vertretern und dem Führer genehm wäre, wobei nicht nur die tschechoslowakische Frage zur Besprechung stünde?

K.H. fragt, was er als eventuelle Besprechungspunkte ausserdem meine.

A.: er könne dies nicht mit Gewissheit sagen, aber er stelle sich vor Luftpakt, Kolonialfrage und Rüstungsabkommen.

K.H. Er wäre die ganze kommende Woche unterwegs und kann vor einer Woche nicht nach Deutschland fahren, auch könne ein solcher Weg nur erwogen werden, wenn dies ein Wunsch der englischen Regierung sei.

A.: Darüber würde er ihm noch Nachricht zukommen lassen, da er voraussichtlich in den nächsten Tagen nach London reise.

Am 23.8. abends rief A. nach einer Besprechung, die Runciman mit Benesch hatte, bei Hohenlohe an und bat ihn für Sonntag, den 28.8., eine Zusammenkunft zwischen Runciman und ihm mit K.H. im Rotenhaus zu arrangieren.

Am 24.8. flog A. nach London ab.

Man trennte sich mit dem gegenseitigen Versprechen eines sehr baldigen Wiedersehens.

Geheime Reichssache!

1. Dies ist eine Geheimsache im Sinne des § 88 R.St.G.B. in der Fassung des Gesetzes vom ...
2. Weitergabe ... b) Postbeförderung ...
3. Empfänger haftet für sichere Aufbewahrung.

Photostatic copy of last page of Document No. 16

No. 17

HITLER'S ORDER FOR REPRISALS AGAINST CZECHOSLOVAKIA[1]

SS REICHSFÜHRER
AND
CHIEF OF GERMAN POLICE
IN THE MINISTRY
OF THE INTERIOR [2]
S V 7.241/38-509-34

Berlin SW 11, September 15, 1938
Prinz-Albrecht-Strasse 8

Express
Secret

Foreign Office,
Berlin

Re: Reprisals against Czechoslovakia

Today, at about 12 noon, the Reichsminister and Head of the Reich Chancellery Dr. Lammers advised by long distance from Obersalzberg that the Führer had approved a proposal he had submitted, viz.:

a) As many Czechoslovak subjects of Czech nationality (including Czech Jews) shall be immediately arrested in the territory of the Reich as Sudeten Germans have been arrested in Czechoslovakia in these past days—approximately since the Führer's speech of September 12, 1938;

---

[1] Document from the Archives of the German Ministry of Foreign Affairs.

[2] Stamp.

b) The Czechoslovak Government shall be informed through the Foreign Office that if death sentences passed on Sudeten Germans are carried out, on each occasion a number of Czechs will be shot in the Reich in reprisal.

I inform you of this order of the Führer for your guidance and action.

I am making inquiries as to the number of Sudeten Germans arrested in Czechoslovakia approximately since September 12, 1938, and have made preparations for the arrest in the territory of the Reich of a corresponding number of Czech subjects of Czech nationality. I request you to inform me immediately the order of the Führer has been communicated to the Czechoslovak Government, and also in case you should learn that death sentences passed on Sudeten Germans have been carried out.

By order,

Signed: *Dr. Best*[1]

---

[1] The document also bears the certifying signature and stamp of the SS Reichsführer.—*Ed*.

No. 18

MEMORANDUM OF VON STECHOW OF THE GERMAN FOREIGN OFFICE[1]

Copy
Berlin, September 15, 1938
S e c r e t [2]

REPORTER: VICE-CONSUL VON STECHOW

Central Office of the Volksdeutsche
Today, by special courier [3]

The Hungarian Minister today visited the Ministry of Foreign Affairs. After the Under Secretary of State had spoken with him of Chamberlain's visit to Obersalzberg, the Minister said that besides the request from his Government which he had communicated by telephone to the Under Secretary of State yesterday, he had received another of a similar nature, namely, that the Sudeten German Party, as such, should not cease to maintain close contact with the

---

[1] Document from the Archives of the German Ministry of Foreign Affairs.

[2] Stamp.

[3] Underscored in the original.—*Ed.*

Hungarian national group, and should keep it constantly informed and act in conjunction with it.

In accordance with the instructions of the Under Secretary of State, I hereby inform the Central Office of the Volksdeutsche of the wish of the Hungarian Minister.

By order,

Signed: *von Stechow*

No. 19

LETTER FROM HIMMLER'S ASSISTANT BEST TO THE GERMAN FOREIGN OFFICE[1]

Berlin SW 11, September 19, 1938
Prinz-Albrecht-Strasse 8

SS REICHSFÜHRER
AND
CHIEF OF GERMAN POLICE
IN THE MINISTRY
OF THE INTERIOR
S-V 7. No. 250/38-509-34

Foreign Office
to be delivered personally to
Legationsrat Freiherr von Heyden-Rynsch,

Berlin, W 8,   *E x p r e s s*
Wilhelmstrasse, 74/76   *S e c r e t*

In supplement to my letter of September 15, 1938,
S-V 7-241/38-509-34

Re: Reprisals against Czechoslovakia

I should appreciate if you would inform me immediately whether the Czechoslovak Government has been apprised of the Führer's order.

---

[1] Document from the Archives of the German Ministry of Foreign Affairs.

As requested, I enclose a list of the 140 arrested Czechoslovak subjects.

The report of the arrest of another ten Czechoslovak subjects in the police district of Liegnitz is not yet to hand.

By order,

Signed: *Dr.Best*[1]

---

[1] The document also bears the certifying signature and stamp of the SS Reichsführer.—*Ed.*

No. 20

LETTER FROM UNDER SECRETARY OF STATE IN THE GERMAN FOREIGN OFFICE WOERMANN TO HIMMLER[1]

Berlin, September 19, 1938

Secret
Express

SS Reichsführer and
Chief of German Police
  in the Ministry
    of the Interior

Reply to letter of 15th inst.
S V 7.241/38-509-34
Reporter: Legationsrat Altenburg

Re: Reprisals against Czechoslovakia

The Czechoslovak Government was apprised of the Führer's order through the German Chargé d'Affaires in Prague on the 17th inst., at 19 h. 20 m.

At the same time, the Legation advises that, press reports notwithstanding, so far there have been no shootings of Sudeten Germans condemned by court martial in Czechoslovakia.

---

[1] Document from the Archives of the German Ministry of Foreign Affairs.

I request that any shooting of Czechoslovak hostages be carried into effect only after preliminary consultation with the Ministry of Foreign Affairs. For that matter, the Führer has to my knowledge reserved it to himself personally to take the decision in this question.

W[1]

---

[1] The document is initialled by Woermann and bears the stamp of the German Ministry of Foreign Affairs.—*Ed*.

No. 21

TELEGRAM FROM CZECHOSLOVAK FOREIGN MINISTER KROFTA TO CZECHOSLOVAK MINISTER IN PARIS OSUSKÝ[1]

Advise the Government and Gamelin, in connection with your last three dispatches, the substance of which is confirmed by information in our possession, which has been transmitted to Paris today by General Faucher, that we believe the pending attack will probably be launched immediately after September 20. We have grave fears that a surprise attack may make it impossible for us to effect mobilization. Nevertheless, we are postponing mobilization, as we consider it undesirable to prejudice the negotiations between Paris and London, and we are loath to do anything that may be regarded in Paris or London as an obstacle to their efforts for the preservation of peace. But we urgently request both the French Government and the French General Staff to recognize the extreme danger of the situation and realize what a responsibility they take upon themselves for our fate and their own, and to inform us as speedily as possible of their view of the situation and to come to our aid as allies and friends.

[1] Published by Z. Fierlinger, in *Ve Službach ČSR* (*In the Service of the Czechoslovak Republic*), Prague, 1947, pp. 154-55. The date of the document is not given.—*Ed.*

I must explain that, in addition to information which unmistakably indicates that there is a plan all ready and timed for a definite date, we are advised that four police regiments are being formed, as was the case in Austria, which are to establish order in the annexed territory after the occupation. According to earlier information, they were being made ready for October 1. We have just intercepted a dispatch dated September 13 in which they are ordered to be in a state of immediate readiness. Parallel with this, a Sudeten German corps, similar to the Austrian legions, is being formed on the frontiers with the help of SS formations. Henlein has just appealed to it to be ready tomorrow near our frontiers. All this indicates that preparations are being made to attack in the next few days. According to our calculations, the attack is to be expected about the 23rd, and we emphasize that the Germans have concentrated in immediate proximity to our frontiers over ten divisions in full fighting readiness and that large numbers of aircraft are being massed; the Germans are repatriating their citizens, while we, counting on Paris and London, dare not take essential preparatory measures for mobilization. We are simultaneously communicating this to Masaryk, but request you to transmit this information yourself to Daladier. We are also informing the French and British Ministers.

No. 22

BRITISH AND FRENCH PROPOSALS TO THE CZECHOSLOVAK GOVERNMENT[1]

THE ANGLO-FRENCH PROPOSALS
PRESENTED TO THE CZECHOSLOVAK
GOVERNMENT ON SEPTEMBER 19, 1938

1. The representatives of the French and British Governments have been in consultation to-day on the general situation, and have considered the British Prime Minister's report of his conversation with Herr Hitler. British Ministers also placed before their French colleagues their conclusions derived from the account furnished to them of the work of his Mission by Lord Runciman. We are both convinced that, after recent events, the point has now been reached where the further maintenance within the boundaries of the Czechoslovak State of the districts mainly inhabited by Sudeten Deutsch cannot, in fact, continue any longer without imperilling the interests of Czechoslovakia herself and of European peace. In the light of these considerations,

---

[1] Published in *Correspondence Respecting Czechoslovakia, September 1938*, London, 1938, No. 7, Cmd. 5847, pp. 8-9.—*Ed.*

both Governments have been compelled to the conclusion that the maintenance of peace and the safety of Czechoslovakia's vital interests cannot effectively be assured unless these areas are now transferred to the Reich.

2. This could be done either by direct transfer or as the result of a plebiscite. We realise the difficulties involved in a plebiscite, and we are aware of your objections already expressed to this course, particularly the possibility of far-reaching repercussions if the matter were treated on the basis of so wide a principle. For this reason we anticipate, in the absence of indication to the contrary, that you may prefer to deal with the Sudeten Deutsch problem by the method of direct transfer, and as a case by itself.

3. The area for transfer would probably have to include areas with over 50 per cent of German inhabitants, but we should hope to arrange by negotiations provisions for adjustment of frontiers, where circumstances render it necessary, by some international body, including a Czech representative. We are satisfied that the transfer of smaller areas based on a higher percentage would not meet the case.

4. The international body referred to might also be charged with questions of possible exchange of population on the basis of right to opt within some specified time-limit.

5. We recognise that, if the Czechoslovak Government is prepared to concur in the measures proposed, involving material changes in the conditions of the State, they are entitled to ask for some assurance of their future security.

6. Accordingly, His Majesty's Government in the United Kingdom would be prepared, as a contribution to the pacification of Europe, to join in an international guarantee of the new boundaries of the Czechoslovak State against unprovoked aggression. One of the principal conditions of such a guarantee would be the safeguarding of the independ-

ence of Czechoslovakia by the substitution of a general guarantee against unprovoked aggression in place of existing treaties which involve reciprocal obligations of a military character.

7. Both the French and British Governments recognise how great is the sacrifice thus required of the Czechoslovak Government in the cause of peace. But because that cause is common both to Europe in general and in particular to Czechoslovakia herself they have felt it their duty jointly to set forth frankly the conditions essential to secure it.

8. The Prime Minister must resume conversations with Herr Hitler not later than Wednesday, and earlier if possible. We therefore feel we must ask for your reply at the earliest possible moment.

No. 23

REPORT OF THE POLISH AMBASSADOR IN BERLIN LIPSKI TO FOREIGN MINISTER BECK[1]

No. 1/165/38 September 20, 1938
Strictly Confidential

M. Minister Beck

Highly Esteemed Minister,

The Chancellor received me today, at 4 p. m., in Obersalzberg, in the presence of Foreign Minister von Ribbentrop. The conversation lasted over two hours.

Prior to this the Chancellor had received the Prime Minister of Hungary and the Hungarian Chief of Staff.

The Polish and the Hungarian audiences were separate. Likewise, whereas the published communiqué on the reception of Premier Imrédy touches on the problems discussed, the communiqué on my audience only mentions the fact that I was received. This was in accordance with my agreement with Foreign Minister von Ribbentrop.

Chancellor Hitler began his talk with me by remarking that developments had taken a different course from what he

---

[1] Original in Polish.

20 września 1938 r.

Najściślej tajne.

Panie Ministrze,

Kanclerz przyjął mnie dziś w Obersalzberg w obecności Ministra Spraw Zagranicznych v. Ribbentropa o godz. 4-tej popołudniu. Rozmowa trwała przeszło dwie godziny.

Uprzednio Kanclerz był przyjął Prezesa Rady Ministrów Węgierskiego oraz szefa sztabu węgierskiego.

Audiencje dla strony polskiej i węgierskiej były udzielone oddzielnie. Również, o ile komunikat prasowy dotyczący przyjęcia Premiera Imredy'ego wchodzi w meritum poruszonych zagadnień, to w komunikacie z mojej audiencji stwierdzony jest jedynie fakt przyjęcia. Uzgodniłem to z Ministrem Spraw Zagranicznych von Ribbentropem.

Kanclerz Hitler rozpoczął swoją ze mną rozmowę od stwierdzenia, iż wypadki poszły inaczej, niż to pierwotnie myślał. Następnie dał zarys historyczny sprawy sudeckiej, począwszy od swojej mowy w Reichstagu w lutym r.b. Podkreślił specjalnie wypadki z 21 maja, które zmusiły go powziąć w dniu 28 maja decyzję dotyczącą wzmocnienia tempa zbrojeń oraz fortyfikacyj na zachodzie. Następnie wskazał na to, iż był do pewnego stopnia zaskoczony propozycją Chamberlaina przyjazdu do Berchtes-

had originally expected. He then made a historical survey of the Sudeten problem, beginning with his speech in the Reichstag in February of this year. He particularly stressed the events of May 21, which had compelled him on May 28 to take the decision to speed up rearmament and fortification in the West. He then said that he was somewhat taken aback by Chamberlain's offer to come to Berchtesgaden. Naturally, it was impossible to refuse to receive the British Premier. He presumed that Chamberlain was coming solemnly to inform him that Great Britain was ready to take armed action. In that case, of course, he would have replied that Germany had reckoned with such a contingency. The Chancellor told Chamberlain that the Sudeten question must be settled, whether by peaceful means or war, in such a way that the Sudetenland was restored to Germany. Chamberlain returned to London convinced by this conversation of the necessity for the severance of the Sudetenland. The Chancellor so far had no explicit information as to what had been decided in London. He likewise still did not definitely know the hour of the meeting which was presumably to take place on the morrow. Nevertheless, information to hand indicated that the Chancellor's demands would be satisfied. True, one version had it that the Sudeten question was not to be settled by self-determination but by a redelimitation of frontiers: that territories where the Germans constitute 80 per cent of the population were to go to Germany without a plebiscite, and that where the percentage was different the possibility of a plebiscite was to be considered. The Chancellor said that he wants a plebiscite, and pronounces in favour of it. He will, of course, insist that persons who left the territory after 1918 should be allowed to vote in the plebiscite. The position of 1918 must be restored. Otherwise it would mean recognizing the Czechization which has taken place since 1918.

The occupation of the Sudetenland by force would, the Chancellor said, be a fuller and more definite solution. Nevertheless, if his conditions were accepted, he could not, if only in face of public opinion in his own country, refuse to accept them, even if the rest of the Czechoslovak problem remained unsettled. The Chancellor was therefore wondering how to solve the remaining part of the problem affecting Hungary and Poland. That was why he had invited the Hungarian Premier and myself for a talk.

Replying, I said that I wanted to present the Polish point of view as broadly as possible. This I did in accordance with points 1-7 of your instructions of September 19, 1938.

For lack of time before dispatching this letter, I will only say that in reference to the Teschen question I twice stressed that what was involved was a territory which only slightly overlapped the Teschen-Freistadt districts, and *access by rail to the Bohumin-Oderberg Station.* [1] In reference to the Hungarian demands, I especially singled out the question of Transcarpathian Rus, laying stress on the strategical factor vis-à-vis Russia, on the communist propaganda carried on in that territory, etc. I got the impression that the Chancellor was very interested in this problem, especially when I told him that the length of the Polish-Rumanian frontier was relatively small, and that by creating a common Polish-Hungarian frontier through Transcarpathian Rus we would erect a wider barrier against Russia. Furthermore, in reference to Transcarpathian Rus, I said that this territory, to which Slovakia did not aspire, was given to Czechoslovakia only by way of mandate, that its population was at a very low level and was strongly mixed, and that it was Hungary that had the biggest interest in it.

---

[1] Underscored in the original.—*Ed.*

Defining our standpoint toward the area directly interesting Poland (Teschen), I stated:

a) that we had made representations to London, Paris, Rome and Berlin categorically demanding a plebiscite, if that is suggested in the case of the Sudetens,

b) that we had yesterday made representations to these same Governments in connection with the report of an alleged project for territorial delimitation (I gave Herr von Ribbentrop our statement in written form),

c) that Poland's position was very strong, because an assurance had been received from Prague, which was confirmed by London and Paris, that our minority in Czechoslovakia would be treated on an equal footing with the most privileged of the other minorities.

In conclusion, in reply to a question of the Chancellor, I said that on this point we would not shrink from resorting to force if our interests were not considered.

Analyzing further the tactics which should be adopted for the solution of the Czechoslovak question as a whole, the Chancellor said:

1. If his proposals were not accepted by Chamberlain, then the position would be clear, and, as he had warned, he was ready to take armed action to annex the Sudetenland to the Reich.

2. If the proposals regarding the Sudetenland were accepted and he were asked to give a guarantee regarding the rest of Czechoslovakia, he would take the stand that he could give a guarantee only if Poland, Hungary and Italy did the same (he regarded the inclusion of Italy as an important counterweight to the French and British guarantee). He realized that Poland and Hungary would not give such guarantees unless the question of their minorities were settled. I assured him of this in the name of the Polish Government.

3. The Chancellor, in utmost confidence, and stressing that I might make due use of it, stated that already today, if a conflict should arise between Poland and Czechoslovakia over our interests in Teschen, the Reich would take our side. (I presume the Chancellor made a similar statement to the Hungarian Premier, although I was not told this.) The Chancellor advises that in such an event we should begin our action only after the Germans had occupied the Sudeten Mountains, because then the whole operation would be much shorter.

In the further course of the conversation the Chancellor insistently stressed that Poland was a factor of prime importance in protecting Europe from Russia.

From the other lengthy statements the Chancellor made, it is to be inferred:

a) that he does not intend to go beyond the territory of the Sudetenland. Of course, in the event of military action he would go farther, because, in my opinion, he would have to yield to the military elements, who, from strategical considerations, are urging him to bring all ethnographic Czechia under German sway;

b) that beyond a definite line of German interests, we have an absolutely free hand;

c) that he foresees great difficulty in securing agreement between Hungary and Rumania. (I think that in this instance the Chancellor was probably influenced by the views of Horthy, of which I informed you orally);

d) that the cost of the Sudeten operation, including fortifications and munitions, amounts to 18 billion marks;

e) that after the Sudeten question is settled he will raise the question of the colonies;

f) that he has conceived the idea of solving the Jewish problem by means of emigration to the colonies, in agreement with Poland, Hungary and perhaps Rumania (to this I replied that if this were done we would raise a splendid monument to him in Warsaw).

Acting on your instruction, I also touched in the course of this conversation on the question of Polish-German relations. I must say that the moment was not very auspicious, since the Chancellor was entirely preoccupied with his forthcoming talk with Chamberlain.

I touched on the question of Danzig, suggesting the possibility of the conclusion of a direct Polish-German treaty to stabilize the position of the Free City.

Here I adduced a number of historical and economic arguments. The Chancellor, in reply, pointed out that we had the treaty of 1934. He also considered it would be desirable to take a further step, and not only preclude the possibility of a resort to force in our mutual relations, but definitively to settle the frontiers. At this point he advanced the suggestion, with which you are already familiar, for a motor highway, connected with the railway. The width of this road, he said, would be about 30 metres. This would in a way be an innovation, in which engineering would serve policy. He said that he was not putting forward the project yet, that it was only an idea, which might be realized later. That being so, I did not go deeper into the question.

At the end of the conversation I mentioned the possibility of arranging a prompt meeting between you and the Chancellor, if it should be necessary. The Chancellor welcomed the idea with pleasure and said that the meeting might be very useful, especially after the talk with Chamberlain.

Ribbentrop, on his part, requested me to ascertain from you whether you might wish to make a statement on the Polish demands on Czechoslovakia, on the lines of that made by the Hungarian Premier, so that it may be utilized in the negotiations with Chamberlain. Furthermore, Ribbentrop assured me that the German press would give the fullest publicity to our actions with regard to our minority in Czechoslovakia.

I am dictating this report just before the departure of the courier after my return by plane from Berchtesgaden, and therefore request you to excuse any inaccuracies.

Accept, etc.,

Jozef Lipski

sty niemieckiej akcja nasza co do mniejszości w Czechosłowacji będzie jak najszerzej uwzględniana.

Powyższe sprawozdanie dyktuję przed wyjazdem kuriera po moim powrocie samolotem z Berchtesgaden. Dlatego zechce Pan Minister uwzględnić możliwe usterki.

Raczy Wielce Szanowny Pan Minister przyjąć wyrazy mego wysokiego poważania i szacunku

/—/ Józef Lipski

No. 24

REPLY OF THE CZECHOSLOVAK GOVERNMENT TO THE ANGLO-FRENCH PROPOSALS[1]

TEXT OF THE REPLY OF
THE CZECHOSLOVAK GOVERNMENT
TO THE ANGLO-FRENCH PROPOSALS,
TRANSMITTED SEPTEMBER 20, 1938

The Czechoslovak Government thank the British and French Governments for the report transmitted, in which they express their opinion on a solution of the present international difficulties concerning Czechoslovakia. Conscious of the responsibility they bear in the interests of Czechoslovakia, her friends and allies and in the interest of general peace, they express their conviction that the proposals contained in the report are incapable of attaining the aims which the British and French Governments expect from them in their great effort to preserve peace.

---

[1] From the Archives of the Ministry of Foreign Affairs of the U.S.S.R. The document was handed by the Czechoslovak Foreign Ministry to the Soviet Plenipotentiary in Prague on September 20, 1938, after the reply had been forwarded to the British and French Governments. It was published by Dr. Hubert Ripka in his *Munich: Before and After*, London, 1939, pp. 74-77.—*Ed.*

These proposals were made without consultation with the representatives of Czechoslovakia. They were negotiated against Czechoslovakia, without hearing her case, though the Czechoslovak Government has pointed out that they cannot take responsibility for a declaration made without their consent. It is hence understandable that the proposals mentioned could not be such as to be acceptable to Czechoslovakia.

The Czechoslovak Government cannot for constitutional reasons take a decision which would affect their frontiers.

Such a decision would not be possible without violating the democratic régime and juridical order of the Czechoslovak state. In any case it would be necessary to consult Parliament.

In the view of the Government, the acceptance of such a proposal would amount to a voluntary and complete mutilation of the state in every respect. Czechoslovakia would be completely paralysed in regard to economics and communications and, from a strategic point of view, her position would become extremely difficult. Sooner or later she would fall under the complete domination of Germany.

Even if Czechoslovakia should make the sacrifices proposed, the question of peace would by no means be solved.

(a) Many Sudeten Germans would, for well-known reasons, prefer to leave the Reich and would settle in the democratic atmosphere of the Czechoslovak state. New difficulties and new nationality conflicts would be the result.

(b) The mutilation of Czechoslovakia would lead to a profound political change in the whole of Central and South-Eastern Europe. The balance of forces in Central Europe and in Europe as a whole would be completely destroyed: it would have the most far-reaching consequences for all other states and especially for France.

(c) The Czechoslovak Government are sincerely grateful to the Great Powers for their intention of guaranteeing the integrity of Czechoslovakia; they appreciate it and value it highly. Such a guarantee would certainly open the way to an agreement between all interested Powers, if the present nationality conflicts were settled amicably and in such a manner as not to impose unacceptable sacrifices on Czechoslovakia.

Czechoslovakia has during recent years given many proofs of her unshakable devotion to peace. At the instance of her friends, the Czechoslovak Government have gone so far in the negotiations about the Sudeten German question that it has been acknowledged with gratitude by the whole world—also a British Government pronouncement stressed that it is necessary not to exceed the bounds of the Czechoslovak Constitution—and even the Sudeten German Party did not reject the last proposals of the Government but publicly expressed its conviction that the intentions of the Government were serious and sincere. In spite of the fact that a revolt has just broken out among a part of the Sudeten population which has been instigated from abroad, the Government have again declared solemnly that they still adhere to the proposals which had met the wishes of the Sudeten German minority. Even to-day they consider this solution as realisable as far as the nationality questions of the republic are concerned.

Czechoslovakia has always remained faithful to her treaties and fulfilled her obligations resulting from them, whether in the interests of her friends or the League of Nations and its members or the other nations. She was resolved and is still resolved to fulfil them under any circumstances. If she now resists the possibility of the application of force, she does so on the basis of recent obligations and declarations of her neighbour and also on the basis of the arbitration treaty of October 16, 1926, which the present German Government have recognised as valid in several pronouncements. The Czechoslovak Government emphasise that this treaty can be applied and ask that this should be done. As they respect their signature, they are prepared to accept any sentence of arbitration which might be pronounced. This would limit any conflict. It would make possible a quick, honourable solution which would be worthy of all interested states.

Czechoslovakia has been always bound to France by respect and most devoted friendship and an alliance which no Czechoslovak Government and no Czechoslovak [1] will ever violate. She has lived and still lives in the belief in the great French nation, whose Government have so frequently assured her of the firmness of their friendship. She is bound to Great Britain by traditional friendship and respect with which Czechoslovakia will always be inspired, by the undissoluble co-operation between the two countries and thus also by the common effort for peace, whatever conditions in Europe prevail.

The Czechoslovak Government appreciate that the effort of the British and French Governments have their source in real sympathy. They thank them for it sincerely. Nevertheless, for reasons already stated, they appeal to them again and for the last time and ask them to reconsider their opinion. They do so in the conviction that they are defending, not only their own interests, but also the interest of their friends, the cause of peace and the cause of healthy development in Europe. At this decisive moment, it is not only a question of the fate of Czechoslovakia, but also the fate of other countries and especially of France.

Prague, September 20, 1938

---

[1] So in the original.—*Ed.*

No. 25

REPLY OF THE BRITISH GOVERNMENT TO THE CZECHOSLOVAK NOTE[1]

September 21, 1938

In the opinion of His Majesty's Government, the reply of the Czechoslovak Government does not meet the critical situation which the Anglo-French proposals were designed to remove and, if it should be adhered to, would lead, after publication, in the opinion of His Majesty's Government, to an immediate German invasion. His Majesty's Government therefore appeals to the Czechoslovak Government to retract their answer and to consider speedily an alternative which would take account of realities. On the basis of the answer submitted, His Majesty's Government would not have any hope in a useful result of the proposed second visit to Herr Hitler and the Prime Minister would be forced to abandon the necessary preparations for it. His Majesty's Government therefore asks the Czechoslovak Government for a speedy and earnest reconsideration before they create a situation for which His Majesty's Government could not take responsibility.

---

[1] Published by Dr. Hubert Ripka in his *Munich: Before and After*, London, 1939, pp. 78-79.—*Ed*.

His Majesty's Government would certainly be ready to submit the Czechoslovak proposal for arbitration to the German Government if they thought that under given circumstances there was any hope of it being favourably considered. But His Majesty's Government cannot believe for a moment that this proposal would be now acceptable and also do not think that the German Government would consider the situation as one which can be repaired by arbitration, as proposed by the Czechoslovak Government.

If the Czechoslovak Government, after reconsideration, would still feel compelled to reject this advice, it must have, of course, complete freedom for any action which it considers appropriate in view of the situation which might develop later.

No. 26

LETTER FROM RUNCIMAN TO CHAMBERLAIN[1]

Westminster, S.W. 1,
September 21, 1938

My dear Prime Minister,

When I undertook the task of mediation in the controversy between the Czechoslovak Government and the Sudeten German party, I was, of course, left perfectly free to obtain my own information and to draw my own conclusions. I was under no obligation to issue any kind of report. In present circumstances, however, it may be of assistance to you to have the final views, which I have formed as a result of my Mission, and certain suggestions which I believe should be taken into consideration, if anything like a permanent solution is to be found.

The problem of political, social and economic relations between the Teuton and Slav races in the area which is now called Czechoslovakia is one which has existed for many centuries with periods of acute struggle and periods of comparative peace. It is no new problem, and in its present

---

[1] Published in *Correspondence Respecting Czechoslovakia, September 1938*, No. 7, pp. 1-8.—*Ed.*

stage there are at the same time new factors and also old factors which would have to be considered in any detailed review.

When I arrived in Prague at the beginning of August, the questions which immediately confronted me were (1) constitutional, (2) political and (3) economic. The constitutional question was that with which I was immediately and directly concerned. At that time it implied the provision of some degree of home rule for the Sudeten Germans within the Czechoslovak Republic: the question of self-determination had not yet arisen in an acute form. My task was to make myself acquainted with the history of the question, with the principal persons concerned, and with the suggestions for a solution proposed by the two sides, viz., by the Sudeten German party in the "Sketch" submitted to the Czechoslovak Government on the 7th June (which was by way of embodying the 8 points of Herr Henlein's speech at Karlsbad), and by the Czechoslovak Government in their draft Nationality Statute, Language Bill, and Administrative Reform Bill.

It became clear that neither of these sets of proposals was sufficiently acceptable to the other side to permit further negotiations on this basis, and the negotiations were suspended on the 17th August. After a series of private discussions between the Sudeten leaders and the Czech authorities, a new basis for negotiations was adopted by the Czechoslovak Government and was communicated to me on the 5th September, and to the Sudeten leaders on the 6th September. This was the so-called 4th Plan. In my opinion—and, I believe, in the opinion of the more responsible Sudeten leaders—this plan embodied almost all the requirements of the Karlsbad 8 points, and with a little clarification and extension could have been made to cover them in their entirety. Negotiations should have at once been resumed on this favourable and hopeful basis; but little doubt remains in my mind that the very fact that they were so favourable operated against their chances, with the more extreme members of the Sudeten German party. It is my belief that the incident arising out of the visit of certain Sudeten German Deputies to investigate into the case of persons arrested for arms smuggling at Mährisch-Ostrau was used in order to provide an excuse for the suspension, if not for the breaking off, of negotiations. The Czech Government, however, at once gave way to the demands of the Sudeten German party in this matter, and preliminary discussions of the 4th Plan were resumed on the 10th September. Again, I am convinced that this did not suit the policy of the Sudeten extremists, and that incidents were provoked and instigated on the 11th September and, with greater effect after Herr Hitler's speech, on the 12th September. As a result of the bloodshed and disturbance thus caused, the Sudeten delegation refused to meet the Czech authorities as had been arranged on the 13th September. Herr Henlein and Herr Frank presented a new series of demands—withdrawal of state police, limitation of troops to their military duties, &c., which the Czechoslovak Government were again prepared to accept on the sole condition that a representative of the party [1] came to Prague to discuss how order should be maintained. On the night of the 13th September this condition was refused by Herr Henlein, and all negotiations were completely broken off.

It is quite clear that we cannot now go back to the point where we stood two weeks ago; and we have to consider the situation as it now faces us.

With the rejection of the Czechoslovak Government's offer on the 13th September and with the breaking off of

---

[1] Sudeten German.—*Ed*.

the negotiations by Herr Henlein, my functions as a mediator were, in fact, at an end. Directly and indirectly, the connection between the chief Sudeten leaders and the Government of the Reich had become the dominant factor in the situation; the dispute was no longer an internal one. It was not part of my function to attempt mediation between Czechoslovakia and Germany.

Responsibility for the final break must, in my opinion, rest upon Herr Henlein and Herr Frank and upon those of their supporters inside and outside the country who were urging them to extreme and unconstitutional action.

I have much sympathy, however, with the Sudeten case. It is a hard thing to be ruled by an alien race; and I have been left with the impression that Czechoslovak rule in the Sudeten areas for the last twenty years, though not actively oppressive and certainly not "terroristic," has been marked by tactlessness, lack of understanding, petty intolerance and discrimination, to a point where the resentment of the German population was inevitably moving in the direction of revolt. The Sudeten Germans felt, too, that in the past they had been given many promises by the Czechoslovak Government, but that little or no action had followed these promises. This experience had induced an attitude of unveiled mistrust of the leading Czech statesmen. I cannot say how far this mistrust is merited or unmerited; but it certainly exists, with the result that, however conciliatory their statements, they inspire no confidence in the minds of the Sudeten population. Moreover, in the last elections of 1935 the Sudeten German party polled more votes than any other single party; and they actually formed the second largest party in the State Parliament. They then commanded some 44 votes in a total Parliament of 300. With subsequent accessions, they are now the largest party. But they can always be outvoted; and consequently some of them feel that constitutional action is useless for them.

Local irritations were added to these major grievances. Czech officials and Czech police, speaking little or no German, were appointed in large numbers to purely German districts; Czech agricultural colonists were encouraged to settle on land transferred under the Land Reform in the middle of German populations; for the children of these Czech invaders Czech schools were built on a large scale; there is a very general belief that Czech firms were favoured as against German firms in the allocation of State contracts and that the State provided work and relief for Czechs more readily than for Germans. I believe these complaints to be in the main justified. Even as late as the time of my Mission, I could find no readiness on the part of the Czechoslovak Government to remedy them on anything like an adequate scale.

All these, and other, grievances were intensified by the reactions of the economic crisis on the Sudeten industries, which form so important a part of the life of the people. Not unnaturally, the Government were blamed for the resulting impoverishment.

For many reasons, therefore, including the above, the feeling among the Sudeten Germans until about three or four years ago was one of hopelessness. But the rise of Nazi Germany gave them new hope. I regard their turning for help towards their kinsmen and their eventual desire to join the Reich as a natural development in the circumstances.

At the time of my arrival, the more moderate Sudeten leaders still desired a settlement within the frontiers of the Czechoslovak State. They realised what war would mean in the Sudeten area, which would itself be the main battlefield. Both nationally and internationally such a settlement would have been an easier solution than territorial transfer. I did my best to promote it, and up to a point with some success, but even so not without misgiving as to whether, when agreement was reached, it could ever be carried out without giving rise to a new crop of suspicions, controversies, accusations and counter-accusations. I felt that any such arrangement would have been temporary, not lasting.

This solution, in the form of what is known as the "Fourth Plan," broke down in the circumstances narrated above; the whole situation, internal and external, had changed; and I felt that with this change my mission had come to an end.

When I left Prague on the 16th September, the riots and disturbances in the Sudeten areas, which had never been more than sporadic, had died down. A considerable number of districts had been placed under a régime called Standrecht, amounting to martial law. The Sudeten leaders, at any rate the more extreme among them, had fled to Germany and were issuing proclamations defying the Czechoslovak Government. I have been credibly informed that, at the time of my leaving, the number of killed on both sides was not more than 70.

Unless, therefore, Herr Henlein's Freikorps are deliberately encouraged to cross the frontier, I have no reason to expect any notable renewal of incidents and disturbances. In these circumstances the necessity for the presence of State Police in these districts should no longer exist. As the State Police are extremely unpopular among the German inhabitants, and have constituted one of their chief grievances for the last three years, I consider that they should be withdrawn as soon as possible. I believe that their withdrawal would reduce the causes of wrangles and riots.

Further, it has become self-evident to me that those frontier districts between Czechoslovakia and Germany where the Sudeten population is in an important majority should be given full right of self-determination at once. If some cession is inevitable, as I believe it to be, it is as well that it should be done promptly and without procrastination. There is real danger, even a danger of civil war, in the continuance of a state of uncertainty. Consequently there are very real reasons for a policy of immediate and drastic action. Any kind of plebiscite or referendum would, I believe, be a sheer formality in respect of these predominantly German areas. A very large majority of their inhabitants desire amalgamation with Germany. The inevitable delay involved in taking a plebiscite vote would only serve to excite popular feelings, with perhaps most dangerous results. I consider, therefore, that these frontier districts should at once be transferred from Czechoslovakia to Germany, and, further, that measures for their peaceful transfer, including the provision of safeguards for the population during the transfer period, should be arranged forthwith by agreement between the two Governments.

The transfer of these frontier districts does not, however, dispose finally of the question how Germans and Czechs are to live together peacefully in future. Even if all the areas where the Germans have a majority were transferred to Germany there would still remain in Czechoslovakia a large number of Germans, and in the areas transferred to Germany there would still be a certain number of Czechs. Economic connexions are so close that an absolute separation is not only undesirable but inconceivable; and I repeat my conviction that history has proved that in times of peace the two peoples can live together on friendly terms. I believe that it is in the interests of all Czechs and of all Germans alike that these friendly relations should be encouraged to re-establish themselves; and I am convinced that this is the real desire of the average Czech and German. They are alike in being honest, peaceable, hardworking and frugal folk. When political friction has been removed on both sides, I believe that they can settle down quietly.

For those portions of the territory, therefore, where the German majority is not so important, I recommend that an effort be made to find a basis for local autonomy within the frontiers of the Czechoslovak Republic on the lines of the "Fourth Plan," modified so as to meet the new circumstances created by the transfer of the preponderantly German areas. As I have already said, there is always a danger that agreement reached in principle may lead to further divergencies in practice. But I think that in a more peaceful future this risk can be minimised.

This brings me to the political side of the problem, which is concerned with the question of the integrity and security of the Czechoslovak Republic, especially in relation to her immediate neighbours. I believe that here the problem is one of removing a centre of intense political friction from the middle of Europe. For this purpose it is necessary permanently to provide that the Czechoslovak State should live at peace with all her neighbours and that her policy, internal and external, should be directed to that end. Just as it is essential for the international position of Switzerland that her policy should be entirely neutral, so an analogous policy is necessary for Czechoslovakia—not only for her own future existence but for the peace of Europe.

In order to achieve this, I recommend:—

(1) That those parties and persons in Czechoslovakia who have been deliberately encouraging a policy antagonistic to Czechoslovakia's neighbours should be forbidden by the Czechoslovak Government to continue their agitations; and that, if necessary, legal measures should be taken to bring such agitations to an end.

(2) That the Czechoslovak Government should so remodel her foreign relations as to give assurances to her neighbours that she will in no circumstances attack them or enter into any aggressive action against them arising from obligations to other States.

(3) That the principal powers, acting in the interests of the peace of Europe, should give to Czechoslovakia guarantees of assistance in case of unprovoked aggression against her.

(4) That a commercial treaty on preferential terms should be negotiated between Germany and Czechoslovakia if this seems advantageous to the economic interests of the two countries.

This leads me on to the third question which lay within the scope of my enquiry, viz., the economic problem. This problem centres on the distress and unemployment in the Sudeten German areas, a distress which has persisted since 1930, and is due to various causes. It constitutes a suitable background for political discontent. It is a problem which exists; but to say that the Sudeten German question is entirely or even in the main an economic one is misleading. If a transfer of territory takes place, it is a problem which will for the most part fall to the German Government to solve.

If the policy which I have outlined above recommends itself to those immediately concerned in the present situation, I would further suggest: (a) That a representative of the Sudeten German people should have a permanent seat in the Czechoslovak Cabinet. (b) That a Commission under a neutral Chairman should be appointed to deal with the question of the delimitation of the area to be transferred to Germany and also with controversial points immediately arising from the carrying out of any agreement which may be reached. (c) That an international force be organised to keep order in the districts which are to be transferred pending actual transfer, so that Czechoslovak State police, as I have said above, and also Czechoslovak troops, may be withdrawn from this area.

I wish to close this letter by recording my appreciation of the personal courtesy, hospitality and assistance which I and my staff received from the Government authorities, especially Dr. Beneš and Dr. Hodža, from the representatives of the Sudeten German party with whom we came in contact, and from a very large number of other people in all ranks of life whom we met during our stay in Czechoslovakia.

Yours very sincerely,
Runciman of Doxford[1]

---

[1] A similar letter was addressed by Lord Runciman on the same day through Masaryk, the Czechoslovak Minister in London, to President Beneš.—*Ed.*

No. 27

MEMORANDUM OF THE CZECHOSLOVAK LEGATION IN MOSCOW TO THE PEOPLE'S COMMISSARIAT OF FOREIGN AFFAIRS OF THE U.S.S.R.[1]

Yesterday, September 21, at 17 h., the following reply of the Czechoslovak Government was communicated to the French and British Ministers in Prague:

1. Under severe duress and extreme pressure of the French and British Governments, the Government of the Czechoslovak Republic accepts with bitterness the Anglo-French proposals, on the presumption that the two Governments will do everything to ensure that in the carrying out of the said proposals the vital interests of the Czechoslovak Republic are safeguarded.[2]

---

[1] The Memorandum was handed by the Czechoslovak Minister in Moscow Fierlinger to Assistant People's Commissar of Foreign Affairs of the U.S.S.R. Potemkin on September 22, 1938. The document is from the Archives of the Ministry of Foreign Affairs of the U.S.S.R.—*Ed*.

[2] The position of the U.S.S.R. on this question may be seen from the telegram sent by the People's Commissar of Foreign Affairs to the Soviet Plenipotentiary in Czechoslovakia on September 20, 1938,

2. The Government of the Czechoslovak Republic notes with grief that it was not even consulted before these proposals were worked out.

The Government regrets that its proposal for arbitration has not been accepted.

The Government accepts the Anglo-French proposals as an indivisible whole and stresses the especial importance it attaches to the promised principle of guarantees.

---

instructing him to communicate to the President of the Czechoslovak Republic the following:

"1) To Beneš' question, whether the U.S.S.R. will, in accordance with the treaty, render immediate and effective aid to Czechoslovakia if France remains loyal to it and also renders aid, you may in the name of the Government of the Soviet Union give an affirmative answer.

"2) You may also give an affirmative answer to Beneš' second question: Will the U.S.S.R. assist Czechoslovakia, as a member of the League of Nations, in accordance with Arts. 16 and 17, if, in the event of attack by Germany, Beneš requests the Council of the League to apply the above-mentioned articles?

"3) Inform Beneš that we are simultaneously advising the French Government of our answer to his two questions."—*Ed.*

No. 28

TELEGRAM FROM UNDER SECRETARY OF STATE IN THE GERMAN FOREIGN OFFICE WOERMANN TO THE GERMAN DIPLOMATIC REPRESENTATIVES IN ROME, WARSAW, BUDAPEST, PRAGUE AND LONDON[1]

Berlin, September 23, 1938

German Diplomatic Representatives in
Rome, No. 318
Warsaw, No. 167
Budapest, No. 162
Prague, No. 256
German Embassy in London, No. 299

CODE TELEGRAM [2]

Urgent [3]

For the personal information of the Chief of Mission:

The negotiations in Godesberg stand at noon today as follows:

The English have conceded the right of self-determination for the Sudeten Germans; there are differences of opinion concerning the modus of cession of the Sudeten German region. The English this morning handed in a note on this subject, which is being answered in writing.

---

[1] Document from the Archives of the German Ministry of Foreign Affairs.

[2] Stamp: "Reported to the Secretary of State."—*Ed.*

[3] In pencil.—*Ed.*

The Hungarian and Polish questions were likewise discussed, but evidently not yet in detail. Our stand is that we give no guarantee for the rest of the State if all the interested States, including Italy, do not share in it, and that we give no guarantee that might prejudice the fate of the other minorities in Czechoslovak territory.

Additional for Rome, Budapest and Warsaw:

The Italian and Polish Ambassadors and the Hungarian Minister have been correspondingly informed by the Reichsminister from Godesberg by telephone.

Woermann[1]

---

[1] The German original bears the notation, "Sent 23.9.38/16¹⁵" and is initialled by Woermann.—*Ed.*

Berlin, den 23. September 1938.

Diplogerma R o m , Nr. ...
     "   W a r s c h a u , Nr. ...
     "   Budapest , Nr. ...
     "   P r a g , Nr. ...
German Embassy L o n d o n , Nr. ...

T e l e g r a m m in Ziffern

(Geh. Ch. Verf.)
Für Missionschef zur persönlichen Information:

Verhandlungen in Godesberg stehen heute mittag folgendermaßen:

Engländer haben Selbstbestimmung für Sudetendeutsche zugestanden, über Modalitäten der Abtrennung sudetendeutschen Gebiets bestehen Meinungsverschiedenheiten. Engländer haben hierüber heute morgen eine Note überreicht, die schriftlich beantwortet wird.

Ungarische und polnische Fragen sind gleichfalls erörtert worden, jedoch anscheinend noch nicht mit Einzelheiten. Wir vertreten Standpunkt, daß wir für Reststaat keine Garantie übernehmen, wenn nicht alle interessierten Staaten einschließlich Italiens daran beteiligt sind, und daß wir keine Garantie übernehmen, die das Schicksal der anderen Minderheiten auf tschechoslowakischem Boden präjudizieren könnte.

                                          Zusatz

Photostatic copy of first page of Document No. 28

Zusatz für Rom, Budapest, Warschau:

Italienischer und Polnischer Botschafter und Ungarischer Gesandter sind von Reichsminister aus Godesberg telefonisch entsprechend unterrichtet worden.

Woermann

No. 29

MINUTE BY SMUTNÝ OF THE TRANSMISSION BY THE BRITISH MINISTER IN PRAGUE NEWTON OF HITLER'S DEMANDS ON CZECHOSLOVAKIA[1]

Mr. Newton, the British Minister, asked me at 8.30 p. m. this evening, September 23, to see him, as he had received important despatches from Godesberg.

In his first letter, of which Mr. Newton gave me a copy, Herr Hitler expresses the opinion that Czechoslovakia is provoking trouble, and that the occupation of the Sudeten German territory by the German Army represents the only possible means of maintaining peace. Herr Hitler describes this proposal as being pacific. If his proposal is not accepted, he gives it to be understood, a military solution will be sought, and that there will be no question of a nationality frontier, but merely of a military and strategic one.

Herr Hitler brought to the first conversation a map of Czechoslovakia, on which the new boundaries were indicated. Mr. Chamberlain objected that these new boundaries

---

[1] Published by Dr. Hubert Ripka in his *Munich· Before and After*, London, 1939, pp. 130-32.—*Ed*.

would give too much territory to Germany, whereupon Herr Hitler declared that he was ready to accept a plebiscite for those parts of the territory which might not be recognised as entirely German. This plebiscite would be conducted two or three months hence under international control, on the model of the plebiscite in the Saar. Any territory which should declare itself in favour of Germany would be occupied immediately by German troops.

Mr. Chamberlain intended to raise certain objections to this second plan of Herr Hitler's at the second conversation, but it seems that this second conversation did not take place, since Mr. Chamberlain informed Herr Hitler of his objections by letter. He said in this letter that he was prepared to submit to the Czechoslovak Government Herr Hitler's proposals regarding the territories in which a plebiscite would be necessary and those in which it would not be necessary. But, Mr. Chamberlain wrote, there was a difficulty in the fact that Herr Hitler was proposing that all the territories should be occupied immediately.

Under these circumstances, it was difficult to continue negotiations, and Mr. Chamberlain expressed doubts whether the plans, worked out by Herr Hitler, would diminish the tension, even if they were accepted. Herr Hitler does not quite understand that Mr. Chamberlain could not propose a plan which would be disapproved by public opinion in England and in France. He is sure that the proposed occupation of these territories by German troops—an action by which these territories would become, for practical purposes, a part of the Reich—would be considered as symbolic. Mr. Chamberlain believes that the Czechoslovak Government would reject a plan of this nature. It would be necessary that Herr Hitler's plan should contain alternatives, to which it would be impossible to raise objections.

If it were desired, Mr. Chamberlain could ask the Czechoslovak Government whether it would be possible to consider, as a practical solution, the transfer to the Sudeten Germans of responsibility for the maintenance of order in those territories about which no doubt was entertained. The Sudeten Germans would create their own organisations in those territories, to replace the German troops, or would make use of organisations which were already in existence, under the control of German observers. Mr. Chamberlain would ask the opinion of the Czechoslovak Government and if Prague accepted this proposal, he would ask the Czechoslovak Government to withdraw their troops and police from the districts in which the Sudeten Germans would maintain order. In his reply to Mr. Chamberlain's letter, Herr Hitler insisted upon his conditions of yesterday. He admitted only one exception, namely, that he would not occupy militarily the territories subject to plebiscite.

Herr Hitler's claims may be summed up as follows:
1. He demands the immediate recall of military and other authorities and of the police from those Sudeten territories which he claims as German.
2. He demands the military occupation of these territories.

Mr. Chamberlain, for his part, demands that Herr Hitler should define his claims in a memorandum, and says that when he has received this memorandum, he will send it to-morrow, by air, to Mr. Newton, the British Minister in Prague. Mr. Chamberlain states to Hitler also, that at the present moment he does not see what more can be done than to send this memorandum and return to London.

Mr. Chamberlain demands at the same time from Herr Hitler a promise that he will not start any military action against Czechoslovak territory until such time as he has received an answer from Prague, as such an action would compromise future negotiations, if such negotiations should take place.

Mr. Newton received first the message about mobilisation (saying that there was no objection to the Czechoslovak mobilisation), and afterwards he received the above information from Godesberg. He is supposed to draw the attention of the Czechoslovak Government to the fact that the announcement of mobilisation might provoke the issue of an immediate order to the German troops to invade Czechoslovakia.

(signed) *Smutný*

No. 30

TRANSMISSION OF HITLER'S DEMANDS ON CZECHOSLOVAKIA BY THE BRITISH MINISTER IN PRAGUE NEWTON[1]

COMMUNICATION OF THE BRITISH MINISTER
OF SEPTEMBER 24, 1938,
RESPECTING HITLER'S MEMORANDUM

On September 24, 1938, at 10 h. 30 m., Minister Newton communicated by telephone the following:

1. He had been informed during the night that the memorandum Hitler handed to Chamberlain would be telegraphed to him. He had not yet received the memorandum.

2. He drew attention to the fact that there were certain amendments to the letter he handed me yesterday, but he could not inform me of them because he had no authorization.

---

[1] In 1938, the People's Commissariat of Foreign Affairs of the U.S.S.R. received through the Soviet Legation in Czechoslovakia a Russian translation of a set of documents which the Czechoslovak Foreign Office intended to publish as a White Paper. The idea was not carried out. This is one of the documents.—*Ed*.

3. He added, in his private capacity, that he considered it very important that no incidents hostile to the Germans should take place in our country just now, that is, that our people should not avenge themselves on German fellow-citizens. I assured Newton that very strict orders had been given on this point, and that the fact that the army was mobilized was the best guarantee that tranquility would be preserved in all circumstances. All the information received by the Ministry from the General Staff and the Ministry of the Interior confirmed that no incidents had taken place, and he could inform London to this effect.

I. Smutný

No. 31

FROM THE CZECHOSLOVAK MINISTER IN LONDON MASARYK TO BRITISH FOREIGN SECRETARY HALIFAX[1]

LETTER FROM THE CZECHOSLOVAK MINISTER IN LONDON TO THE SECRETARY OF STATE FOR FOREIGN AFFAIRS

London, September 26, 1938

Sir,

I have communicated to my Government the Prime Minister's question which he put to me yesterday afternoon and for which he wished an answer. This question of the Prime Minister's, as I understood it, I transmitted to Prague as follows:—

"Although Herr Hitler did say that the memorandum handed to the Czechoslovak Government by His Majesty's Government was his last word, and although Mr. Chamberlain doubts very much that he could induce Herr Hitler to change his mind at this late hour, the Prime Minister may, under circumstances, make a last effort to persuade Herr Hitler to consider another method of settling peacefully the Sudeten German question,

[1] Published in *Correspondence Respecting Czechoslovakia, September 1938*, London, 1938, No. 7, pp. 18-19.—*Ed.*

namely, by means of an international conference attended by Germany, Czechoslovakia and other Powers which would consider the Anglo-French plan and the best method of bringing it into operation. He asked whether the Czechoslovak Government would be prepared to take part in this new effort of saving the peace."

To this question I have now received the following answer of my Government:—

"The Czechoslovak Government would be ready to take part in an international conference where Germany and Czechoslovakia, among other nations, would be represented, to find a different method of settling the Sudeten German question from that expounded in Herr Hitler's proposals, keeping in mind the possible reverting to the so-called Anglo-French plan. In the note which Mr. Masaryk delivered to Mr. Chamberlain yesterday afternoon, mention was made of the fact that the Czechoslovak Government, having accepted the Anglo-French note under the most severe pressure and extreme duress, had no time to make any representations about its many unworkable features. The Czechoslovak Government presumes that, if a conference were to take place, this fact would not be overlooked by those taking part in it."

My Government, after the experiences of the last few weeks, would consider it more than fully justifiable to ask for definite and binding guarantees to the effect that no unexpected action of an aggressive nature would take place during the negotiations, and that the Czechoslovak defence system would remain intact during that period.

I have, &c.,
Jan Masaryk

No. 32

REPORT OF THE POLISH AMBASSADOR IN BERLIN LIPSKI TO FOREIGN MINISTER BECK[1]

Copy

No. 1/172/38

September 26, 1938
Strictly Confidential

Minister of Foreign Affairs,
    Warsaw

I have the honour to supplement the two telegrams sent you today respecting the morning conversations with Secretary of State Weizsäcker and Minister of Foreign Affairs von Ribbentrop with the following information:

What exactly took place at the conference in Godesberg it was very hard to ascertain, since until today Minister von Ribbentrop and Secretary of State Weizsäcker were away from Berlin.

Moreover, the world press was full of false rumours which led observers there astray.

Under these circumstances, the sole authoritative document was the German memorandum—result of the Godesberg conference—which was communicated to the Berlin representatives of Poland, Hungary and Italy. I had the honour to transmit it to you with my letter of the 24th inst., No. 1/171/38.

---

[1] Original in Polish.

I would only mention that on the second day of the conference in Godesberg, Herr von Ribbentrop, about 1 o'clock in the afternoon, informed me that the Chancellor had declined the proposal for a pact of non-aggression and a guarantee for Czechoslovakia, of which I immediately informed you by telegraph.

Among the Polish press representatives in Godesberg (Director Dembiński of PAT) the version was confidentially imparted by the British that the crisis in Godesberg arose because of the Chancellor's demand that the Czechoslovak problem be settled at once in its entirety, including the Polish and Hungarian demands.

The tension is supposed to have been relieved during the night, in the decisive conversation between Chamberlain and the Chancellor, when the latter withdrew that demand.

The Hungarian Minister when he visited me this morning also intimated that in his last conversation with Chamberlain the Chancellor yielded to British pressure, which was expressed, among other things, in the British Premier's declaration that he would have to leave Godesberg the next day.

The Hungarian Minister believes that the Chancellor's decision was also influenced by the pressure of German military spheres, who feared an international conflagration, and by the opinion of high officials in the Foreign Ministry, who, as I have been able to verify, are constantly warning of the possibility of action by England and France. In the light of information received, the Hungarian Minister expressed the fear that the Czech Government, while accepting the German memorandum now, will later revert to the pact of non-aggression, not, however, for the whole territory of Czechoslovakia, but only for the sector of the new German-Czech delimitation, and that the Chancellor, under British pressure, may agree to it. I told the Hungarian

26 września 1938 r.

N/1/172/38.
Załącznik do No.Dz.:

Najściślej tajne.

Dwa telegramy, wysłane w dniu dzisiej-
szym na skutek rozmów rannych z Sekretarzem Stanu Weiz-
säckerem oraz Ministrem Spraw Zagranicznych von Ribbentropem, mam zaszczyt uzupełnić następującymi wiadomo-
ściami.

Zorientowanie się ścisłe co do istotne-
go przebiegu konferencji w Godesbergu było nad wyraz
utrudnione wskutek nieobecności w Berlinie aż do dnia
dzisiejszego zarówno Ministra von Ribbentropa jak i
Sekretarza Stanu Weizsäckera.

Poza tym prasa międzynarodowa przepeł-
niona była fałszywymi pogłoskami, wprowadzającymi w błąd
tamtejszych obserwatorów.

W tym stanie rzeczy jedynym miarodajnym
dokumentem, który powstał w rezultacie konferencji, było zakomunikowane tutejszym przedstawicielem Polski,
Węgier i Włoch memorandum niemieckie, które miałem zaszczyt przesłać Panu Ministrowi przy piśmie z dnia 24
b.m. Nr. N/1/171/38.

Przypomnę tylko, że w drugim dniu obrad

Do
Pana Ministra Spraw Zagranicznych

w W a r s z a w i e

Minister that I considered this out of the question, since Hitler in his conversation with me at Berchtesgaden had clearly defined his position in this matter.

After this meeting with the Hungarian Minister, I had a talk in the Foreign Office, first with Herr Weizsäcker, and then with Herr von Ribbentrop.

From what they told me I gather that in the negotiations in Godesberg the Chancellor confined himself to discussing solely the Sudeten problem. He proceeded from the premise that to raise the problem in its entirety at the present juncture would only complicate the matter. Indirectly, however, the Polish and Hungarian questions were touched on when the Chancellor rejected the proposal for a pact of non-aggression and a guarantee. Ribbentrop told me that the Chancellor rejected the pact of non-aggression on the ground that in the hands of the Czechs it would be an instrument directed against the aspirations of the Polish and Hungarian minorities. The guarantee was rejected by the Chancellor on the ground that he would have to make it conditional on guarantees being given also by Poland, Hungary and Italy. Ribbentrop added that the British Government does not particularly insist on a guarantee, apparently because, in the view of traditional British policy, guarantees are undesirable.

An interesting remark with regard to guarantees was made by Weizsäcker, who said that he would not be surprised if Beneš renounced a guarantee from other countries and demanded it only of France and England, and made it a condition for the acceptance of the German memorandum.

In answer to my question, what exactly had caused the tension at Godesberg, Ribbentrop said that after the talk at Berchtesgaden, Chamberlain strove to lend the transfer of the Sudetenland a form that would be more acceptable to public opinion in the West. This would corroborate the information sent you after the talk with Woermann that Chamberlain's greatest objection was to Germany's demand for military occupation of the territory by October 1. Nevertheless, Ribbentrop authorized me, with the request not to divulge it to anyone else, to inform you that Chamberlain personally promised the Chancellor to make every effort to get the memorandum put into effect. This, of course, could not be told to the outside world, and that is why the statement appeared in the communiqué that the British Premier would transmit the memorandum to the Czech Government.

In Ribbentrop's reception room I met the British and Italian Ambassadors. The British Ambassador only had time to tell me that he considered the situation critical. The Italian Ambassador, on the basis of information received from Rome, expressed the fear that Chamberlain's position was becoming very ticklish. From this I gathered that Mussolini fears the British Premier may vacillate. The Italian Ambassador told me that, on Mussolini's instructions, he had come to see Ribbentrop with the purpose of exerting influence not to have Hitler aggravate the situation in his speech today. He would recommend that Hitler should say that he was prepared to give a guarantee, making it dependent on Czechoslovakia's neighbours (Poland and Hungary) and on Italy.

I asked Ribbentrop whether the Chancellor in his speech today would touch upon the whole Czechoslovak problem, to which he replied that he was not yet acquainted with the contents of the speech and that he intended to talk with the Chancellor today.

From Weizsäcker's more definite statements and from Ribbentrop's vaguer ones, it follows that until the Sudeten problem is solved Hitler will have to concentrate all his attention on it. Nevertheless, Ribbentrop assured me that

Hitler definitely stood for the satisfaction of the Polish and Hungarian demands.

Then Ribbentrop declared in a rather general way that he saw two possibilities:

1. Either the Czech Government accepts the memorandum, and then the peaceful occupation of the territory would ensue. In that case he suggested whether we should not come together and discuss our further line in the Polish and Hungarian questions. I answered evasively that, as we had already said in Berchtesgaden, it is possible that you may meet the Chancellor.

The other possibility, as Herr von Ribbentrop sees it, is the eventual necessity of a German invasion. He asked whether we would invade too under these circumstances. I replied that I could naturally not express an opinion on this question since that was for the Government to decide.

Strictly in my own name, I said that if our demands were not satisfied resort to force was not precluded, whether Germany invaded the territory or whether she occupied it peacefully.

Already toward the end of the conversation Herr von Ribbentrop said that from operational considerations it would be well, in case of necessity, to maintain contact, to which I made no answer.

Herr von Ribbentrop said that he would always be at my disposal at any moment and considered direct contact very desirable, and that if anything important should transpire from the talks with Wilson he would let me know immediately.

Ambassador of the Polish Republic,
Jozef Lipski

No. 33

REPORT OF THE POLISH AMBASSADOR IN BERLIN LIPSKI TO FOREIGN MINISTER BECK[1]

Copy

EMBASSY OF THE
POLISH REPUBLIC
BERLIN
No. 1/182/38

Strictly Confidential
September 27, 1938

Minister of Foreign Affairs,
    Warsaw

I. Today, at 7 o'clock, I was invited by Secretary of State Weizsäcker to the Foreign Office for a talk, after which, on Herr von Ribbentrop's invitation, I had a talk with him.

Herr von Weizsäcker informed me of the results of Sir Horace Wilson's talk with the Chancellor today, and read me the stenographic report.

In this conversation, the Chancellor took the stand that the Czech Government must accept the memorandum, and declared that he would not depart from this position.

In the course of the conversation, Sir Horace Wilson defined the possibility of England's taking action against

---

[1] Original in Polish.

Ambasada R.P. Berlin

N/1/152/38.

27 września 1938 r.

Najściślej tajna.

I. W dniu dzisiejszym zaprosił mnie na rozmowę do Auswärtiges Amt sekretarz stanu p. Weizsäcker o godz. 7-ej, następnie na zaproszenie p. von Ribbentropa odbyłem z nim rozmowę.

P. von Weizsäcker poinformował mnie o rezultacie dzisiejszej rozmowy Sir Horace Wilsona z Kanclerzem, przy czym odczytał stenogram. Kanclerz w rozmowie tej stanął na stanowisku, iż memorandum musi być przyjęte przez Rząd Czeski i to on z tego stanowiska się nie cofnie. W trakcie rozmowy Sir Horace Wilson w ten sposób — cytuję stenogram dosłownie — określił możliwe wystąpienie Anglii przeciwko Niemcom: "Wenn die Tschechoslowakei das Memorandum ablehnt, wisse man nicht, wo die Sache ende. Wenn Deutschland die Tschechoslowakei angreift, so würde Frankreich der Tschechoslowakei gegenüber ihre vertraglichen Verpflichtungen erfüllen. Wenn dieser Fall eintrete und dabei die französischen Streitkräfte in Feindseligkeiten mit Deutschland verwickelt werden — ob dies eintreten würde, wisse er nicht — dann wird sich England verpflichtet fühlen, Frankreich Hilfe zu leisten." P. von Weizsäcker wyjaśnił że Wilson przeczytał te słowa, zaznaczając, iż oddaje wiernie myśl Chamberlaina.

Do
Pana Ministra Spraw Zagranicznych
W a r s z a w a

Photostatic copy of first page of Document No. 33

Germany as follows (I quote verbatim from the stenographic report):

"If Czechoslovakia were to reject the memorandum, it was not known how the matter would end. If Germany should attack Czechoslovakia, France would carry out her contractual obligations toward Czechoslovakia. In that event, and should France's armed forces be involved in hostilities with Germany—whether this would happen, he did not know—then England would feel obliged to render assistance to France." [1]

Herr von Weizsäcker said that Wilson stressed these words and stated that he was conveying Chamberlain's thought faithfully.

I said to Weizsäcker that this formula was typical of British policy. Herr Weizsäcker remarked that in the course of the conversation Wilson referred to the possibility of an Anglo-German understanding on a number of questions. He also, evidently, strongly emphasized the necessity to avoid a catastrophe. As far as I gathered, at the end of the conversation he said he would act in this direction.

Herr von Ribbentrop, with whom I talked after this, believes that the British Government will still bring very strong pressure to bear on Prague to get it to accept the memorandum. To my inquiry whether tomorrow's date and hour—2 p. m.—still held good, the Secretary of State replied he had asked me to keep all this an absolute secret precisely in order that this date should not become known anywhere. It is therefore subject to change.

II. Then, in conformity with your telegram of yesterday, I informed both the Foreign Minister and the Secretary of State of the course of our negotiations with Prague,

---

[1] The quotation in inverted commas from the stenographic report is given in the original in German.—*Ed.*

stressing that we would not allow ourselves to be caught in a trap and would demand concrete adjustments.

III. Herr von Weizsäcker, with a General Staff map before him, said that he would suggest that tomorrow our Military Attaché, together with a competent Staff officer, trace the demarcation line on the map, in order, in the event of hostilities, that there might be no collision between our armed forces.

I said to Herr von Weizsäcker that I first considered it necessary to establish with him the territory of our political interests in Czechoslovakia. Since Herr von Weizsäcker did not have such a map with him, we agreed that we would discuss this question early tomorrow morning. The question of the delimitation of the spheres, in case of necessity, by the military experts has been temporarily postponed.

IV. When the talk with the Secretary of State passed to general subjects, we touched upon the position of France and England.

Herr Weizsäcker said that, unfortunately, his department was poorly informed of the position of France, since French Ambassador François-Poncet had not set foot in the Foreign Office for nearly a fortnight, and was getting his information from another source, and that Ambassador Welczek was away from Paris. The Secretary of State, however, noted a considerable stiffening of French public opinion.

V. Herr von Ribbentrop, in the course of the general exchange of opinions, stressed the belief, to which I referred above, that the English side would bring very strong pressure to bear upon Prague. He thinks that the British Government will do everything in its power to settle the question peacefully and not let it come to an armed conflict. He reckons with the possibility of a local conflict. He does not, however, preclude the possibility of a general conflict, for which he is prepared. Referring to my earlier talks with him, I spoke of the importance of localizing the conflict.

As to Russia, Herr von Ribbentrop is rather optimistic.

Asked by Herr von Ribbentrop whether Poland would take armed action if the memorandum were executed in a peaceful way, I replied that I could not predetermine the position of my Government.

Then Herr von Ribbentrop touched on the hypothesis that the Czechs would not accept the memorandum, and then, as he put it, Czechia would be destroyed. He asked casually whether in that case we would take action, and at what moment. I was able to gather from Herr von Ribbentrop's words that he thinks that, since the main concern of the Polish Government is the Eastern frontier, it will take part in a conflict only after it has become clear whether it is of a local character or a world war. In the event of the occupation of all Czechoslovakia by Germany, Herr von Ribbentrop thinks it would be useful if the political and military interests were more specifically defined. He requested that I draw your special attention to this and receive instructions.

VI. 1) In conclusion, I have the honour to state that further talks on the German memorandum are already pointless, since the Chancellor definitely fixed his position in the conversation with Wilson.

2) I request you, after consultation with the General Staff, to send me instructions in regard to the Secretary of State's concrete proposal to define the demarcation line on the territory of our interests in the Teschen district,

3) also instructions in regard to Ribbentrop's suggestion concerning the eventuality of hostilities and Germany's crossing the line of her direct interests in Czechoslovakia.

Ambassador of the Polish Republic,

Jozef Lipski

No. 34

COMMUNICATION OF THE GERMAN DELEGATION IN MUNICH TO THE GERMAN FOREIGN OFFICE ON THE COURSE OF THE MUNICH CONFERENCE[1]

Secret

Munich, September 29, 1938
19 h. 00 m.

For the Under Secretary of State in the Foreign Office, Berlin
To be delivered by special messenger!

Immediately! *Immediately!*

The Under Secretary of State
to acknowledge receipt

Strictly Secret!

The Führer opened the conference at 12:45 and expressed his thanks to the attending Heads of Governments for having accepted his invitation to Munich. He added that he wanted first of all to give a brief outline of the Czech question as it stood at the present moment. The existence of Czechoslovakia in its present form was threatening European peace. The German, Hungarian, Slovak, Polish and Carpatho-Russian minorities, who were forced into this State against their will, revolted against its continued existence. He, the Führer, could only speak for the German minority.

---

[1] Document from the Archives of the German Ministry of Foreign Affairs.

Geheime Reichssache

Ausfertigung

236

München, den 29. September 1938
19 :00 Uhr.

Für Unterstaatssekretär Auswärtiges Amt, Berlin

Durch besonderen Boten abtragen!

S o f o r t !   S o f o r t !

Empfangsbestätigung des Unterstaatssekretärs hierher.

S t r e n g g e h e i m !

Der Führer eröffnete um 12.45 Uhr die Besprechungen und sprach den erschienenen Regierungschefs seinen Dank dafür aus, daß sie seiner Einladung nach München gefolgt seien. Er fügte hinzu, er wolle zunächst einen kurzen Abriß der tschechischen Frage, wie sie sich augenblicklich darstelle, geben. Die Existenz der Tschechoslowakei bedrohe in ihrer gegenwärtigen Gestalt den europäischen Frieden. Die deutschen, ungarischen, slowakischen, polnischen und karpathorussischen Minderheiten, die gegen ihren Willen in diesen Staat hineingepreßt worden seien, revoltierten gegen das Fortbestehen dieses Staates. Er, der Führer, könne nur als Sprecher für die deutschen Minderheiten auftreten.

Im Interesse des europäischen Friedens müsse das Problem in der kürzesten Frist gelöst werden, und zwar durch die Einlösung des von der Tschechischen Regierung abgegebenen Versprechens der Übergabe. Deutschland könne dem Jammer und Elend der sudetendeutschen Bevölkerung nicht länger zusehen. In zunehmendem Maße liefen Nachrichten über Zerstörung von Eigentum ein

Die

Photostatic copy of first page of Document No. 34

In the interest of peace in Europe this problem must be solved without the slightest delay, namely, by the fulfilment of the promise given by the Czech Government to transfer [the territory]. Germany could not stand by and watch the misery and poverty of the Sudeten German population any longer. Reports of the destruction of property were coming in in increasing number. The population was being barbarously persecuted. Since he, the Führer, had last spoken with Mr. Chamberlain, the number of refugees had risen to 240,000, and there seemed to be no end to the flow. Furthermore, it was necessary to put an end to the political, military and economic tension, which was unbearable. This tension demanded that the problem should be settled within a few days, for it was no longer possible to wait weeks. At the request of the Head of the Italian Government, he, the Führer, had expressed his willingness to postpone mobilization in Germany for twenty-four hours. Further procrastination would be criminal. The responsible statesmen of Europe had gathered here to settle the problem, and he noted that the differences were minimal, because, first, all were agreed that the territory must be ceded to Germany, and, second, that Germany claimed nothing more than this territory. It could not be left to a commission to make an exact definition of the territory in question. This required a plebiscite, all the more so since free elections had not been held in Czechoslovakia for twenty years. He had declared in his speech in the Sportpalast that on the first of October he would march in [1] (einmarschieren werde) whatever happened. To this it was replied that such procedure would bear the character of an act of violence. The task, consequently, was to deprive the act of this character. Action, however, must be taken

---

[1] To Czechoslovakia.—*Ed.*

immediately, first, because the persecutions could no longer be contemplated with indifference, and also because, in view of the vacillations in Prague, further delay could not be tolerated. From the military standpoint, the occupation presented no problem, since the depth to be penetrated was on all sides small. Given the desire, therefore, it would be possible to evacuate the territory in ten days, even, he was convinced, in six or seven days. In deference to British and French public opinion, he would leave the question open whether German troops should also march into the territory where the plebiscite is to be held. But in that case there must be a position of parity, the Czechs must do the same. The modus of the transfer could be discussed, but action must be taken quickly. That armed Powers should stand facing each other in Europe, as they were now, could not be tolerated for long.

Prime Minister Chamberlain began by thanking the Führer for the invitation to the conference. He also thanked the Duce, to whose initiative, if he understood correctly, today's conference was due. This conference gave Europe a new respite, whereas yesterday catastrophe seemed imminent. He quite agreed that swift action must be taken, and he especially welcomed the Führer's statement that he did not want to resort to force, but to establish order. If the problem were approached in this spirit, he was certain that results would be achieved.

The Head of the Italian Government said that they all were already agreed in theory, and the thing now was to translate theory into practice. The time factor was particularly important. Every delay was a source of danger. He particularly insisted on expeditious action, because here expedition accorded with justice. It would be better to come to an agreement this very day, for a delay of even twenty-four hours would cause new uneasiness and new suspicion.

By way of a practical solution of the problem, he would like to make the following proposal (see Enclosure 1).[1]

French Prime Minister Daladier likewise thanked the Führer for his initiative. He was glad to have the opportunity to meet him personally. There had been plans for such a meeting before, but circumstances had unfortunately prevented it until now. But, as the French proverb said, better late than never.

Prime Minister Daladier then addressed the Duce and expressed his especial admiration at his step, which, it was to be hoped, would lead to a solution of the problem. Like Mr. Chamberlain, he was of the opinion that action must be taken with the greatest speed. He particularly welcomed the objectivity and realism of the Duce's proposal, which he accepted as a basis for discussion. This of course did not mean that he agreed to all points, since the economic aspects ought to be taken into account, in order not to create a soil for future wars. Lastly, there was the question of the organization of the plebiscite and the delimitation of the zone. He mentioned these points only because he had not yet studied the proposal just read. But he could accept it right away as a basis for discussion.

Prime Minister Chamberlain likewise welcomed the Duce's proposal and declared that he himself had pictured the solution along the same lines. As to the guarantee which was being asked of Britain, he would be glad if a representative of the Czech Government were present. For England could naturally not give any guarantee that the territory would be evacuated by October 10 and that no destruction would take place, unless an assurance were given to this effect by the Czech Government.

The Führer replied to this that he was not interested in

---

[1] The enclosure is missing from the file.—*Ed.*

assurances from the Czech Government, as it was precisely this government that was doing the destruction. The question was how the Czech Government could be made to accept the proposal. There was unanimity that the territory was to be ceded to Germany. The Czechs, however, declared that they could not evacuate it until new fortifications had been built and economic decisions taken.

Prime Minister Daladier said that the French Government would under no circumstances tolerate dilatory conduct on the part of the Czech Government. The Czech Government had given its word, and it must keep it. There could be no question of postponing the evacuation of the territory until new fortifications had been built. He requested this idea to be excluded from the discussion altogether, since the Czech Government would receive a guarantee in return for its concessions. Nevertheless, like Mr. Chamberlain, he was of the opinion that the presence of a Czech representative who could be consulted if necessary would be useful. It seemed to him useful, above all else, in order to avert disorders, which in so delicate a matter as the cession of territory might easily arise. Everything should be done to avoid chaos.

To this the Führer replied that if the Czech Government was to be asked for its consent to every detail, a settlement could not be expected before fourteen days. The Duce's proposal envisaged the setting up of a commission which would include a representative of the Czech Government. What he was interested in above all was a guarantee from the Great Powers, who must use their authority to make the Czech Government stop the persecution and destruction.

Prime Minister Chamberlain said that he too did not think the matter should be delayed any longer. But before he could give a guarantee he had to know whether he could honour it, and he would therefore welcome it if a representative of the Prague Government were present in the next room from whom he could receive assurances.

The Führer replied that there was no Czech representative with authority to speak for his Government here at the moment. What he was interested in knowing was what would happen if the Czech Government did not accept the proposal of the Great Powers. Two hundred and forty-seven bridges and an even greater number of houses had already been destroyed.

The Italian Prime Minister said that he likewise did not think they could wait for a Czech representative. The Great Powers must assume a moral guarantee for the evacuation and for the prevention of destruction. They must tell Prague that the Czech Government must accept the demands, otherwise it must bear the military consequences. What was needed was a request by the Great Powers, whose moral duty it was that this territory shall not be a wilderness when it is turned over.

Prime Minister Chamberlain replied that he would very much like to have a Czech representative present. For the rest, the time limits proposed by the Duce seemed to him quite reasonable. He was prepared to subscribe to them, and to inform the Czech Government that it ought to accept them. But he could not give any guarantee until he knew how he could honour it. Besides, there were still a few points that had to be cleared up. What would be the powers of the international commission, and what regime would prevail in the territory after it had been evacuated? He had no doubt that the Führer would see that order was maintained and also take care that those inhabitants who were opposed to the Anschluss would not be persecuted. But there were certain points in the German memorandum which were not understood in England. It was asked, for instance, what was the meaning of the condition that no cattle were to be removed from this territory. Did it mean that the farmers would be deported, but that their cattle would remain?

The Führer replied that it went without saying that German law would operate in the territory to be ceded to Germany. At present, however, the very opposite was the case: the Czechs were carrying off the cattle of the German farmers. The decisive thing it seemed to him was: was the question regarded as a German-Czech conflict which would be settled in fourteen days, or as a problem of European significance. If it was a European problem, then the Great Powers must throw their authority into the scales and assume responsibility for seeing to it that the transfer was carried out properly. If the Czech Government did not accept these proposals, it would be clear that the greatest moral authority, which in general must exist, namely, the authority embodied in the signatures of the four statesmen here assembled, was not sufficient. In that case the question could be settled only by resort to force.

Prime Minister Chamberlain said that he had no objections to raise to the proposed time limits. The Czech question was a European question, and the Great Powers had not only the right, but the duty to settle it. They also had to see to it that the Czech Government did not refuse, out of perverseness or obstinacy, to evacuate the territory. He wanted the authority of the Great Powers to be applied properly, and he therefore suggested that the Duce's plan should first be distributed and the meeting adjourned for a short while in order that the plan might be studied. This would involve no delay.

Prime Minister Daladier said that he had already taken upon himself the responsibility in London, when, without asking the Czech Government, he had given his consent in principle to the cession of the German areas. He had taken

Die tschechische Frage sei eine europäische Frage, und die Großmächte hätten sie zu lösen nicht nur das Recht, sondern auch die Pflicht. Sie hätten auch dafür zu sorgen, daß die Tschechische Regierung nicht aus Unvernunft und Hartnäckigkeit die Räumung ablehne. Er habe den Wunsch, die Autorität der Großmächte in der richtigen Weise anzuwenden, und darum habe er vor, den Plan des Duce zunächst zu verteilen und die Sitzung auf kurze Zeit zu unterbrechen, damit dieser Plan studiert werden könne. Ein solches Verfahren bedeute keine Verzögerung.

Ministerpräsident Daladier führte aus, daß er bereits seine Verantwortung in London übernommen habe, als er, ohne die Tschechische Regierung zu fragen, aus Prinzip die Abtretung des deutschen Gebiets angenommen habe. Er habe diesen Standpunkt eingenommen, obwohl Frankreich einen Bündnisvertrag mit der Tschechoslowakei habe. Falls die Zuziehung eines Prager Vertreters Schwierigkeiten mache, sei er bereit, darauf zu verzichten, denn es komme darauf an, daß die Frage schnell gelöst werde.

Der F ü h r e r erwiderte hierauf, daß, wenn ein Dokument mit den Unterschriften der vier Staatsmänner trotzdem von der Prager Regierung abgelehnt werde, letzten Endes Prag nur die Gewalt respektiere.

Angenommen: Heinisch.

Photostatic copy of last page of Document No. 34

this stand even though France had a treaty of alliance with Czechoslovakia. If it should be difficult to secure the participation of a representative of Prague, he was prepared not to insist upon it, since the important thing was to have the question settled quickly.

To this the Führer replied that if a document bearing the signatures of the four statesmen were rejected by the Prague Government, this would mean that Prague in the end only respected force.

Received: *Heinisch*

No. 35

TEXT OF MUNICH AGREEMENT[1]

AGREEMENT BETWEEN GERMANY,
THE UNITED KINGDOM,
FRANCE AND ITALY
CONCLUDED AT MUNICH
ON SEPTEMBER 29, 1938

Germany, the United Kingdom, France and Italy, taking into consideration the agreement which has been already reached in principle for the cession to Germany of the Sudeten German territory, have agreed on the following terms and conditions governing the said cession and the measures consequent thereon, and by this agreement they each hold themselves responsible for the steps necessary to secure its fulfilment—

1. The evacuation will begin on the 1st October.

2. The United Kingdom, France and Italy agree that the evacuation of the territory shall be completed by the 10th October, without any existing installations having been destroyed and that the Czechoslovak Government will be held responsible for carrying out the evacuation without damage to the said installations.

3. The conditions governing the evacuation will be laid down in detail by an international commission composed

---

[1] Published in *Further Documents Respecting Czechoslovakia*, Miscellaneous No. 8, 1938, Cmd. 5848.—*Ed.*

Geheime Reichssache
Abkommen

zwischen Deutschland, dem Vereinigten Königreich, Frankreich und Italien, getroffen in München, am 29. September 1938.

Deutschland, das Vereinigte Königreich, Frankreich und Italien sind unter Berücksichtigung des Abkommens, das hinsichtlich der Abtretung des sudetendeutschen Gebiets bereits grundsätzlich erzielt wurde, über folgende Bedingungen und Modalitäten dieser Abtretung und über die danach zu ergreifenden Massnahmen übereingekommen und erklären sich durch dieses Abkommen einzeln verantwortlich für die zur Sicherung seiner Erfüllung notwendigen Schritte.

1.) Die Räumung beginnt am 1.Oktober.

2.) Das Vereinigte Königreich, Frankreich und Italien vereinbaren, dass die Räumung des Gebiets bis zum 10.Oktober vollzogen wird, und zwar ohne Zerstörung irgendwelcher bestehender Einrichtungen, und dass die Tschechoslowakische Regierung die Verantwortung dafür trägt, dass die Räumung ohne Beschädigung der bezeichneten Einrichtungen durchgeführt wird.

3.)

Photostatic copy of first page of German text of Munich Agreement of September 29, 1938

7.) Es wird ein Optionsrecht für den Übertritt in die abgetretenen Gebiete und für den Austritt aus ihnen vorgesehen. Die Option muss innerhalb von sechs Monaten vom Zeitpunkt des Abschlusses dieses Abkommens an ausgeübt werden. Ein deutsch-tschechoslowakischer Ausschuss wird die Einzelheiten der Option bestimmen, Verfahren zur Erleichterung des Austausches der Bevölkerung erwägen und grundsätzliche Fragen klären, die sich aus diesem Austausch ergeben.

8.) Die Tschechoslowakische Regierung wird innerhalb einer Frist von vier Wochen vom Tage des Abschlusses dieses Abkommens an alle Sudetendeutschen aus ihren militärischen und polizeilichen Verbänden entlassen, die diese Entlassung wünschen. Innerhalb derselben Frist wird die Tschechoslowakische Regierung sudetendeutsche Gefangene entlassen, die wegen politischer Delikte Freiheitsstrafen verbüssen.

München, den 29. September 1938.

Ed Daser Mussolini Neville Chamberlain

Photostatic copy of last page of German text of Munich Agreement of September 29, 1938

of representatives of Germany, the United Kingdom, France, Italy and Czechoslovakia.

4. The occupation by stages of the predominantly German territory by German troops will begin on the 1st October. The four territories marked on the attached map will be occupied by German troops in the following order: The territory marked No. I on the 1st and 2nd of October, the territory marked No. II on the 2nd and 3rd of October, the territory marked No. III on the 3rd, 4th and 5th of October, the territory marked No. IV on the 6th and 7th of October. The remaining territory of preponderantly German character will be ascertained by the aforesaid international commission forthwith and be occupied by German troops by the 10th of October.

5. The international commission referred to in paragraph 3 will determine the territories in which a plebiscite is to be held. These territories will be occupied by international bodies until the plebiscite has been completed. The same commission will fix the conditions in which the plebiscite is to be held, taking as a basis the conditions of the Saar plebiscite. The commission will also fix a date, not later than the end of November, on which the plebiscite will be held.

6. The final determination of the frontiers will be carried out by the international commission. This commission will also be entitled to recommend to the four Powers—Germany, the United Kingdom, France and Italy—in certain exceptional cases minor modifications in the strictly ethnographical determination of the zones which are to be transferred without plebiscite.

7. There will be a right of option into and out of the transferred territories, the option to be exercised within six months from the date of this agreement. A German-Czechoslovak commission shall determine the details of the

option, consider ways of facilitating the transfer of population and settle questions of principle arising out of the said transfer.

8. The Czechoslovak Government will within a period of four weeks from the date of this agreement release from their military and police forces any Sudeten Germans who may wish to be released, and the Czechoslovak Government will within the same period release Sudeten German prisoners who are serving terms of imprisonment for political offences.

Adolf Hitler
Édouard Daladier
Benito Mussolini
Neville Chamberlain

Munich, September 29, 1938

ANNEX TO THE AGREEMENT

His Majesty's Government in the United Kingdom and the French Government have entered into the above agreement on the basis that they stand by the offer, contained in paragraph 6 of the Anglo-French proposals of the 19th September, relating to an international guarantee of the new boundaries of the Czechoslovak State against unprovoked aggression.[1]

When the question of the Polish and Hungarian minorities in Czechoslovakia has been settled, Germany and Italy for their part will give a guarantee to Czechoslovakia.

(Same signatures)

Munich, September 29, 1938

---

[1] See Document No. 22.—*Ed.*

Zusatz zu dem Abkommen.

Seiner Majestät Regierung im Vereinigten Königreich und die französische Regierung haben sich dem vorstehenden Abkommen angeschlossen auf der Grundlage, daß sie zu dem Angebot stehen, welches im Paragraph 6 der englisch-französischen Vorschläge vom 19.September enthalten ist, betreffend eine internationale Garantie der neuen Grenzen des tscechischslovakischen Staates gegen einen unprovozierten Angriff.

Sobald die Frage der polnischen und ungarischen Minderheiten in der Tschechoslowakei geregelt ist, werden Deutschland und Italien Ihrerseits der Tschechoslowakei eine Garantie geben.

München, den 29.September 1938.

Neville Chamberlain
Mussolini
Ed. Daladier

Photostatic copy of German text of Annex to Munich Agreement of September 29, 1938

Zusätzliche Erklärung.

Die Regierungschefs der vier Mächte erklären, daß das Problem der polnischen und ungarischen Minderheiten in der Tschechoslowakei, sofern es nicht innerhalb von drei Monaten durch eine Vereinbarung unter den betreffenden Regierungen geregelt wird, den Gegenstand einer weiteren Zusammenkunft der hier anwesenden Regierungschefs der vier Mächte bilden wird.

München, 29.September 1938.

Photostatic copy of German text of the Supplementary Declaration to the Munich Agreement of September 29, 1938

COMPOSITION OF THE INTERNATIONAL COMMISSION

The four Heads of Government here present agree that the international commission provided for in the agreement signed by them today shall consist of the Secretary of State in the German Foreign Office, the British, French and Italian Ambassadors accredited in Berlin, and a representative to be nominated by the Government of Czechoslovakia.

(Same signatures)

Munich, September 29, 1938

SUPPLEMENTARY DECLARATION

All questions which may arise out of the transfer of the territory shall be considered as coming within the terms of reference to the international commission.

(Same signatures)

Munich, September 29, 1938

DECLARATION

The Heads of the Governments of the four Powers declare that the problems of the Polish and Hungarian minorities in Czechoslovakia, if not settled within three months by agreement between the respective Governments, shall form the subject of another meeting of the Heads of the Governments of the four Powers here present.

(Same signatures)

Munich, September 29, 1938

No. 36

KORDT'S MINUTE OF THE MUNICH CONFERENCE[1]

Copy
Secret

MINUTE OF THE MUNICH CONFERENCE
4 h. 30 m., September 29, 1938

On the recommendation of the Duce it was first decided to discuss the Italian proposal submitted to the delegations in the morning point by point. Point 1 (the evacuation to begin on October 1) was accepted unanimously.

On point 2 the Führer said that if agreement could also be reached on this point, the question of the modus of the evacuation would not give rise to big difficulties. His proposal was that first the definite stages of the German occupation should be marked on the map; the modus could then be determined by a commission, which would include a Czech representative.

Prime Minister Chamberlain said that he agreed with the time limit laid down in point 2, October 10, for the completion of the evacuation of the German territory. He, however, expressed doubt whether he could give Germany a guarantee so long as he did not know what the attitude of Czechoslovakia was to the question of evacuation.

---

[1] Document from the Archives of the German Ministry of Foreign Affairs.

Abschrift.

Geheime Reichssache

A u f z e i c h n u n g

über die Münchener Besprechung um 4 Uhr 30
am 29. September 1938.

Auf Vorschlag des Duce wurde zunächst beschlossen, den am Vormittag den Delegationen zugestellten italienischen Vorschlag Punkt für Punkt zu besprechen. Zunächst wurde Punkt 1) (Beginn der Räumung am 1.10) einstimmig angenommen.

Zu Punkt 2) führte der Führer aus daß, falls auch über diesen Punkt Einverständnis erzielt werden könne, die Frage der Modalitäten keine großen Schwierigkeiten mehr bereiten würde. Sein Vorschlag gehe dahin, zunächst auf der Karte gewisse Etappen der deutschen Besetzung festzulegen, deren Modalitäten alsdann in einer Kommission, in der auch ein tschechischer Vertreter sitzen werde, festgelegt werden könnten.

Min.Präs. Chamberlain erklärte sich mit dem in Punkt 2) festgelegten Datum der Beendigung der Räumung des deutschen Gebiets, dem 10.Oktober, einverstanden. Er äußerte jedoch Zweifel über die Möglichkeit, eine Garantie an Deutschland zu geben, solange er nicht wisse, wie die Tschechoslowakei sich zur Räumungsfrage verhalte.

Zu der Frage, ob für die Gewährung der im italienischen Vorschlag vorgesehenen Garantie die vorherige Zustimmung der Tschechoslowakei eingeholt werden müßte, so wie es Mr.Chamberlain anzuregen schien, äußerte sich Daladier dahingehend, daß ihm eine derartige Zustimmung nicht notwendig erschiene.

Er

Photostatic copy of first page of Document No. 36

On the question whether it was necessary to request the consent of Czechoslovakia before giving the guarantee envisaged in the Italian proposal, as Mr. Chamberlain seemed to wish, Daladier said that he did not think such consent was necessary. He, when in England,[1] had consented in principle to the cession of the territory by Czechoslovakia, without first inquiring of the Czechoslovak Government, in spite of the existence of the Franco-Czech pact, and his opinion now was that once the promise had been given, it should be kept. Daladier also rejected, in view of the Anglo-French guarantee, the Czechoslovak objection, mentioned in the course of the discussion, that the evacuation could take place only when the erection of new fortifications on Czech territory had been completed. The evacuation of the purely German area could therefore be effected quickly; difficulties would only arise where there were enclaves. In these districts, it seemed to him, international occupation by British, Italian and French troops would be expedient. In addition, it was necessary, in his opinion, as a supplement to the Wilsonian principle of self-determination, to take geographical, economic and political realities into account. Furthermore, in the case of the enclaves, the principle of exchange of populations practised in Greece, Turkey, Bulgaria and Poland could also be applied.

The Führer said he agreed that districts with disputable majorities should not be occupied by German troops, but should be first occupied by international military units. If point 2 were accepted, he was prepared to be generous with regard to the delimitation of the territory. The theory advanced by M. Daladier that economic, geographical and political factors must be taken into account when

---

[1] The original has "an England," which is an obvious misprint.—*Ed.*

defining the frontiers seemed to him dangerous, because it was precisely to this theory that the Czechoslovak State owed its origin in 1918. At that time an entity was created which was viable economically, but not viable nationally. Moreover, economic difficulties could more easily be settled than national difficulties, all the more that Czechoslovakia, not being a nation with an old culture, could not assimilate the German population.

After a lengthy discussion of the different meanings of the word "guarantee" in England and on the continent, the point was referred to a drafting committee for reformulation. This committee, after long deliberation, drew up the preamble contained in the text of the treaty, and reformulated point 2.

From this moment on the conference dissolved into individual discussions, dealing in particular, with the help of maps, with the zones due to be evacuated and the districts where the plebiscite is to be held. In the course of these discussions Daladier suggested the exchange of a large zone with a predominantly German population on the Silesian border, in which there were Czech fortifications, for a corresponding Czech strip of land in the Bohemian Forest, remarking that the presence of Czech fortifications was not the sole reason for the suggestion, but that he also had political and psychological considerations in mind.

The Führer declined this suggestion in view of the purely German character of the area in question, but after long negotiation agreed to accept the formula embodied in the treaty regarding modifications of the frontiers (see point 6 of the Munich Agreement).

Daladier expressed his warm thanks to the Führer for this, and declared that the adoption of this formula would make his position in France much easier. On return-

auszusprechen habe, so tue er dies auch gleichzeitig im Namen des deutschen Volkes.

Chamberlain erwiderte im Namen der ausländischen Staats= männer und schloß sich den Ausführungen des Führers über die Zufriedenheit der betroffenen Völker mit dem Münchener Ergebnis an. Er unterstrich im übrigen die Bedeutung des Abkommens für die Weiterentwicklung der europäischen Politik.

gez. Erich Kordt.

Photostatic copy of last page of Document No. 36

ing to France he would say that the Führer made this personal gesture to him (Daladier).

The agreements reached in the individual discussions of the statesmen were then finally formulated by a four-power drafting committee, with the assistance of the legal advisers of the delegations, and were given a first reading at about ten o'clock in the evening. The final text of the treaty was ready by about eleven o'clock, and between eleven and twelve o'clock it was signed in four languages. At the same time the conference adopted a supplementary declaration on the settlement of the problem of the Polish and Magyar minorities on the basis of a proposal made by Mussolini; a supplementary agreement concerning a guarantee to be given for the new frontiers of the Czech State; a supplementary declaration to the effect that all questions arising in connection with the transfer of territory came within the terms of reference to the international commission which was to be set up; and another supplementary declaration on the composition of the international commission in Berlin.

In conclusion, the Führer thanked the foreign statesmen for having accepted his invitation to the four-power conference in Munich and for their efforts for the happy outcome of the negotiations. Both the German people and the other peoples concerned would hail this outcome with the greatest joy, and in expressing his thanks he also did so in the name of the German people.

Chamberlain replied on behalf of the foreign statesmen and associated himself with the Führer's conviction that the Munich decision would be greeted with satisfaction by the nations concerned. He also stressed the importance of the agreement for the future course of European policy.

Signed: *Erich Kordt*

No. 37

A CZECHOSLOVAK FOREIGN MINISTRY RECORD OF THE CZECHOSLOVAK DELEGATION'S VISIT TO MUNICH[1]

MADE IN MUNICH BY DR. HUBERT MASAŘÍK,
at 4 a. m., September 30, 1938

At 3 p. m. on September 29, 1938, our airplane took off from Ruzyn. After eighty minutes' flight we landed at Munich. The reception we met with at the airdrome was roughly that accorded to police suspects. We were taken in a police car, accompanied by members of the Gestapo, to the Hotel Regina, where the British Delegation was also staying. The Conference was already in progress and it was difficult to establish any contact with leading members either of the British or French delegations. Nevertheless I called out by telephone first Mr. Rochat and then Mr. Ashton-Gwatkin. The latter told me he wished to speak to me immediately in the Hotel.

At 7 p. m. I had my first conversation with Mr. Ashton-Gwatkin. He was nervous and very reserved. From certain cautious remarks, I gathered that a plan, the details of which Mr. Gwatkin could not then give me, was already completed in its main outlines and that it was much harsher

---

[1] Published by Dr. Hubert Ripka in his *Munich: Before and After*, London, 1939, pp. 224-27.—*Ed.*

than the Anglo-French proposals. On our red map, I explained to him all our really vital interests. Mr. Gwatkin showed a certain understanding in the question of the Moravian corridor, though he completely ignored all the other elements of the problem.

According to him, the Conference should end at the latest tomorrow, Saturday. Up to now, only Czechoslovakia had been discussed. I drew Mr. Gwatkin's attention to the consequences of such a plan from the internal political, economic and financial aspect. He answered that I did not seem to realize how difficult the situation was for the Western Powers or how awkward it was to negotiate with Hitler. On which, Mr. Gwatkin returned to the Conference, promising that we should be called at the first interval.

At 10 p. m. Mr. Gwatkin took Dr. Mastný and myself to Sir Horace Wilson. There, in the presence of Mr. Gwatkin and at the express wish of Mr. Chamberlain, Sir Horace told us the main lines of the new plan and handed us a map on which were marked the areas which were to be occupied at once. To my objections, he replied twice with absolute formality that he had nothing to add to his statements. He paid no attention whatever to what we said concerning places and areas of the greatest importance to us. Finally, he returned to the Conference and we remained alone with Mr. Gwatkin. We did what we could to convince him of the necessity of revising the plan. His most important reply was that made to M. Mastný, to the effect that the British Delegation favoured the new German plan.

When he again began to speak of the difficulties of negotiating with Hitler, I said that, in fact, everything depended on the firmness of the two Western Great Powers. To which Mr. Gwatkin answered in a very serious tone: "If you do not accept, you will have to settle your affairs all alone with the Germans. Perhaps the French will put it more amiably, but I assure you that they share our views. They will disinterest themselves. . . ."

At 1:30 a. m. we were taken into the hall where the Conference had been held. There were present Mr. Neville Chamberlain, M. Daladier, Sir Horace Wilson, M. Léger, Mr. Ashton-Gwatkin, Dr. Mastný and myself. The atmosphere was oppressive; sentence was about to be passed. The French, obviously embarrassed, appeared to be aware of the consequences for French prestige. Mr. Chamberlain, in a short introduction, referred to the agreement which had just been concluded and gave the text to Dr. Mastný to read out. During the reading of the text, we asked the precise meaning of certain passages. Thus, for example, I asked MM. Léger and Wilson to be so kind as to explain the words "preponderantly German character" in Article 4. M. Léger, without mentioning a percentage, merely remarked that it was a question of majorities calculated according to the proposals we had already accepted. Mr. Chamberlain also confirmed that there was no question except of applying a plan which we had already accepted. When we came to Article 6, I asked M. Léger whether we were to consider it as a clause assuring the protection of our vital interests as had been promised in the original proposals. M. Léger said, "Yes," but that it was only possible to a very moderate degree, and that the question would come under the International Commission. Dr. Mastný asked Mr. Chamberlain whether the Czechoslovak member of the commission would have the same right to vote as the other members, to which Mr. Chamberlain agreed. In answer to the question whether international troops or British forces would be sent to the plebiscite areas, we were told that that was under consideration, but that Italian and Belgian troops might also participate.

While M. Mastný was speaking with Mr. Chamberlain about matters of perhaps secondary importance (Mr. Chamberlain yawned without ceasing and with no show of embarrassment), I asked MM. Daladier and Léger whether they expected a declaration or answer to the agreement from our Government. M. Daladier, obviously embarrassed, did not reply. M. Léger replied that the four statesmen had not much time. He added positively that they no longer expected an answer from us; they regarded the plan as accepted and that our Government had that very day, at latest by 5 p. m. to send its representative to Berlin to the meeting of the International Commission and finally that the Czechoslovak official whom we sent would have to be in Berlin on Saturday, in order to fix the details of the evacuation of the first zone. The atmosphere was becoming oppressive for everyone present.

It had been explained to us in a sufficiently brutal manner, and that by a Frenchman, that this was a sentence without right of appeal and without possibility of modification.

Mr. Chamberlain did not conceal his fatigue. After the text had been read, we were given a second slightly corrected map. We said "Good-bye" and left. The Czechoslovak Republic as fixed by the frontiers of 1918 had ceased to exist. In the hall I met Rochat, who asked me what the reactions would be at home. I replied curtly that I did not exclude the worst and that it was necessary to be prepared for the gravest eventualities.

No. 38

TRANSMISSION OF THE MUNICH DEMANDS BY THE GERMAN CHARGÉ D'AFFAIRES IN PRAGUE HENCKE TO CZECHOSLOVAK FOREIGN MINISTER KROFTA[1]

MINUTE
OF THE TRANSMISSION OF THE GERMAN
NOTIFICATION OF THE MUNICH DECISIONS

On September 30, 1938, at 5 a.m., the German Legation telephoned a request of the Chargé d'Affaires to be received before 6 o'clock by Foreign Minister Krofta, to whom he would communicate the decision of the Munich conference of the four Great Powers. He arrived at 6:15, and the Foreign Minister made the following minute of his visit:

"Hencke transmitted the Munich decision together with a letter inviting our representative to be in Berlin today at 17 o'clock. He said that the map would be delivered by the British Legation. He had not been instructed to add any-

---

[1] Original in Czech. Document from the Archives of the Czechoslovak Foreign Ministry (see footnote to Document No. 30). The minute was made by Minister Ina, General Secretary of the Czechoslovak Foreign Ministry.—*Ed.*

thing to the letter. He only remarked that, in his opinion, there was no difference between Berchtesgaden and Godesberg."

Meanwhile Minister Krno arrived at the Ministry, together with Dr. Čremák and Minister Smutný. Foreign Minister Krofta spoke over the telephone with Prime Minister General Syrový, while Minister Smutný informed the President of the Republic. The President invited the leaders of the political parties to come and see him at half past nine. The Cabinet met at the Kolovrat Palace, and later— together with seven political leaders, representatives of the political parties, and generals—in the office of the President of the Republic.

In the forenoon, the French, British and Italian Ministers requested Minister Krno to arrange for Foreign Minister Krofta to receive them in order that they might learn from him the decision of the Government. They wanted to know the decision before noon. But as the Foreign Minister returned from the President only at 12, the Ministers could not be received before 12:30. They entered the Foreign Minister's office in a body, and he said to them:

"On behalf of the President of the Republic and of the Government, I declare that we submit to the decisions adopted in Munich without us and against us. Our point of view will be communicated to you in writing. At present I have nothing to add. I only desire to draw your attention to the necessity of persuading the German Government that the campaign against us which has been going on for several weeks in the press and by radio must cease at once, otherwise it will be impossible to carry out the program established at Munich in a peaceful way." [1]

Minister de Lacroix did not conceal that he agreed with

---

[1] In the original this statement is in French.—*Ed*.

the Foreign Minister's statement that the decision had been taken "against us," and said that Daladier expressed in this connection "ses vifs regrets." Newton averred that Chamberlain had done all he could for us. Franzoni said nothing. The Minister closed the talk with the following words:

"I do not want to criticize, but for us this is a catastrophe which we have not deserved. We submit, and will try to secure a tranquil life for our people. I do not know whether your countries will benefit from this decision taken at Munich, but certainly we shall not be the last. After us, others will meet with the same fate."

September 30, 1938

No. 39

ANGLO-GERMAN DECLARATION[1]

JOINT DECLARATION BY
ADOLF HITLER AND
NEVILLE CHAMBERLAIN

Munich, September 30, 1938

We, the German Führer and Chancellor and the British Prime Minister, have had a further meeting today and are agreed in recognizing that the question of Anglo-German relations is of the first importance for the two countries and for Europe.

We regard the agreement signed last night and the Anglo-German Naval Agreement as symbolic of the desire of our two peoples never to go to war with one another again.

We are resolved that the method of consultation shall be the method adopted to deal with any other questions that may concern our two countries, and we are determined to continue our efforts to remove possible sources of difference and thus to contribute to assure the peace of Europe.

Adolf Hitler, Neville Chamberlain

---

[1] Published in *Times*, October 1, 1938, p. 12.—*Ed.*

No. 40

LETTER FROM KEITEL TO WEIZSÄCKER[1]

OBERKOMMANDO OF THE
WEHRMACHT
No. 2576/38. Secr. L. Ia.

Copy
Berlin, W. 35,
October 10, 1938
Secret

Foreign Office,
For Secretary of State Dr. Weizsäcker,
Berlin

Re: Situation in Iglau

The Oberkommando of the Wehrmacht requests you to demand from the Czechoslovak Government and the International Commission the immediate provision of adequate protection for the Germans living in Brünn and Iglau, and to inform these towns accordingly.

The Führer agrees to the employment of the British Legion, should it be transferred to Czechoslovakia, for the protection of the Germans especially in Brünn and Iglau.

---

[1] Document from the Archives of the German Ministry of Foreign Affairs. It bears a pencil note: "Original received 10:10 from the Secretary of State with notification to send it to the Reichsminister."—*Ed.*

Abschrift.

Oberkommando der Wehrmacht.　　　　　　　　Berlin W.35, den 10. Okt. 1938.

Nr. 2576/38 geh. L I a

Geheim.

Betr: Lage in Jglau.

Bezug: D-R.Min.d.J. I S 9.10.38.

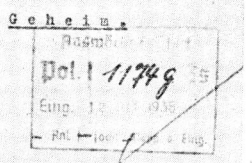

An das
　　　　　Auswärtige Amt,
　　　　　z.Hd. Herrn Staatssekretär Dr. Weizsäcker.

Berlin.

Das Oberkommando der Wehrmacht bittet, bei der Tschechischen Regierung und dem Internationalen Ausschuß die sofortige Sicherstellung eines ausreichenden Schutzes für die Deutschen in Brünn und Jglau zu verlangen und diese Städte entsprechend zu benachrichtigen.

Der Führer ist damit einverstanden, daß die englische Legion, falls sie in die Tschechoslowakei transportiert werden sollte, zum Schutz der Deutschen besonders in Brünn und Jglau eingesetzt wird.

Sollte die Lage in Brünn und Jglau für die dort wohnenden Deutschen bedrohlichen Charakter annehmen, so ist damit zu rechnen, daß der Führer den sofortigen Einmarsch deutscher Truppen in diese Gebiete befiehlt.

　　　　　　　　Der Chef des Oberkommandos der Wehrmacht.
　　　　　　　　gez: Keitel.

Ich bemerke hierzu, daß wir heute früh bereits entsprechende Schritte in Prag unternommen haben. Wegen der Behandlung der Sache beabsichtige ich bald mit dem General Keitel direkt zu sprechen. Hiermit dem
　　　　　Herrn Reichsminister
vorzulegen.
　　　　　Berlin, den 10. Oktober 1938.

Photostatic copy of Document No. 40

If the situation in Brünn and Iglau should become *menacing*[1] to the Germans living there, the fact must be reckoned with that the Führer will give orders for the immediate entry of German troops into these areas.

Chief of the High Command of the Wehrmacht,
Signed: *Keitel*

I add hereto that we have this morning taken corresponding steps in Prague. I intend soon to speak directly with General Keitel regarding the handling of the matter.

Submit this to the Reichsminister
Berlin, October 10, 1938 [2]

---

[1] Underscored in the original.—*Ed*.
[2] Below the date there is Altenburg's signature in pencil.—*Ed*.

No. 41

TELEPHONE MESSAGE FROM GODESBERG TO SECRETARY OF STATE WEIZSACKER[1]

TELEPHONE MESSAGE FROM GODESBERG
Received 16 h. 45 m.
Polit. I No. 1198
Secret[2]

NOTE FOR THE SECRETARY OF STATE

In his conversation with the Reichsminister of Foreign Affairs in Godesberg on October 11, the Führer decided the following:

I

The German side will make no demand for a plebiscite in any other district of Czechoslovakia.

II

The underlying tendency of our further line respecting the International Commission shall be to strive to have the International Commission disappear from the scene as quickly as possible, and as early as possible to replace it by direct bilateral negotiations with Czechoslovakia.

---

[1] Document from the Archives of the German Ministry of Foreign Affairs.
[2] Stamp.

Telefonat aus Godesberg
aufgen. um 16,45 Uhr

Auswärtiges Amt
Pol. I 1198 g Rs
Eing. 17 Okt. 1938

Aufzeichnung

für den Herrn Staatssekretär.

Der Führer hat in seinem Gespräch mit dem Herrn Reichsaußenminister am 11. Oktober in Godesberg folgendes entschieden:

I.

Von deutscher Seite sollen keine weiteren Gebiete der Tschechoslowakei für eine Volksabstimmung gefordert werden.

II.

Als Grundtendenz für die weitere Einstellung gegenüber der Internationalen Kommission ist das Ziel zu verfechten, die Internationale Kommission so rasch wie möglich zum Verschwinden zu bringen und an ihre Stelle möglichst bald direkte zweiseitige Verhandlungen mit der Tschechoslowakei zu setzen.

III.

Die endgültige Festlegung der Grenzen in der Internationalen Kommission soll so rasch wie möglich erfolgen. Die Festlegung der tatsächlichen Grenzen an Ort und Stelle soll dann später ausschließlich einer deutsch-tschechischen Grenzkommission übertragen werden.

IV.

Die Internationale Kommission soll beschließen, daß alle mit einer Option zusammenhängenden Fragen der unmittelbaren Regelung Deutschlands mit der Tschechoslowakei übertragen werden.

(Von dem zuständigen Ressort soll geprüft werden, ob eine Ausweisung der 27 000 Juden tschechischer Staatsangehörigkeit aus Wien möglich ist.)

V.

Es ist das Ziel zu erstreben, von den Tschechen die Genehmigung zum Bau einer Reichsautobahn, die der Bahnlinie Breslau-Zwittau-Brünn-Wien folgen soll, unter gleichzeitiger Internationalisierung dieser Bahnlinie zu erhalten. Den Tschechen sollen hierfür dieselben Privilegien hinsichtlich der Internationalisierung der Bahnlinie, die die Zwittauer Halbinsel durchschneidet, unter gleichzeitiger

Photostatic copy of first page of Document No. 41

III

The definitive establishment of the frontiers by the International Commission must take place as quickly as possible. The establishment of the actual frontiers on the spot shall then be referred exclusively to a German-Czech frontier commission.

IV

The International Commission shall decide that all questions connected with option are subject to direct settlement between Germany and Czechoslovakia.

(The appropriate department shall examine the possibility of deporting from Vienna the 27,000 Czech Jews.)

V

Efforts must be made to secure the consent of the Czechs to the building of a motor highway [1] running parallel to the Breslau-Zwittau-Brünn-Vienna railway, and the internationalization of this railway. The Czechs shall be offered in return similar privileges with regard to the internationalization of the railway intersecting the Zwittau peninsula,[2] as well as the right to build a motor highway. Ambassador Ritter shall sound out the Economic Commission on this matter.

VI

The standpoint of Germany regarding the transfer of the property of state enterprises and public utilities in the ceded territories, as well as the restitution of property removed therefrom, shall be unconditionally upheld.

---

[1] In the original: "Reichsautobahn."—*Ed.*
[2] So in the original; the reference is to the frontier salient.—*Ed.*

VII

It must be most energetically declared from the very beginning that there must be no doubt that Germany will never assume any share of the Czech national debt, inasmuch as this debt was incurred by Czechoslovakia with the purpose of fighting Germany.[1]

VIII

As regards the question of Mährisch-Ostrau and Witkowitz, the Secretary of State shall invite the Polish Ambassador to see him and declare to him the following:

While not interested in Oderberg, Germany is interested in Mährisch-Ostrau and Witkowitz. The question whether Mährisch-Ostrau and Witkowitz shall be left to the Czechs will depend on further developments. If the future of these regions is brought up for discussion, then we shall demand a plebiscite under international control.

IX

As to Pressburg, for the time being absolute reserve shall be exercised and all questions connected with this problem shall be thoroughly examined. If the Hungarians should approach us with demands on Pressburg, they shall be told the following:

a) Germany's attitude toward the Hungarian claims on Czechoslovakia is in principle sympathetic.

b) The Führer has repeatedly declared that Germany can draw the sword only in behalf of German interests.

c) The Führer had invited the Hungarian Prime Minister and Foreign Minister to Obersalzberg and advised them to push their cause somewhat more energetically. But in

---

[1] In the original: "zwischen Deutschland."—*Ed.*

dort den Rat erteilt, etwas energischer ihre Sache zu vertreten. Die Ungarn haben aber in den darauffolgenden kritischen Tagen nichts getan, daraus erkläre sich ihre gegenwärtige schwierige diplomatische Lage.

d.) Was die gegenwärtigen tschechisch-ungarischen Verhandlungen betreffe, so ist der Standpunkt, daß einwandfreie national-ungarische Gebiete an Ungarn zu fallen haben; auch Deutschland habe keine strategischen Grenzen errichtet, sondern nur Volkstumsgrenzen.

e.) Wenn irgendwelche Differenzen bestehen bleiben, so müsse eine Abstimmung unter internationaler Kontrolle erfolgen.

X.

Zur persönlichen Informierung des Staatssekretärs.

Sollte Ungarn mobilisieren, so liege es nicht in unserer Absicht, den Ungarn in den Arm zu fallen und ihnen etwa einen Rat auf Mäßigung zu geben.

Godesberg, den 12. Oktober 1938

- - - - -

Photostatic copy of last page of Document No. 41

the crucial days that followed the Hungarians did nothing, and this explains their present diplomatic predicament.

d) As to the present Czech-Hungarian negotiations, our standpoint is that territories with unquestionably preponderating Hungarian populations should be ceded to Hungary; Germany, too, had established, not strategical, but only national frontiers.

e) Where differences remain unsettled, there must be a plebiscite under international control.

X

For the personal information of the Secretary of State.

If Hungary should mobilize, it is not our intention to hinder the Hungarians or to advise them to display moderation.

Godesberg, October 12, 1938

No. 42

FRANCO-GERMAN DECLARATION[1]

M. Georges Bonnet, Minister of Foreign Affairs of the French Republic, and M. Joachim von Ribbentrop, Minister of Foreign Affairs of the German Reich, acting in the name and by order of their respective Governments, have agreed on the following points at their meeting in Paris on December 6, 1938;

1) The French Government and the German Government fully share the conviction that pacific and neighbourly relations between France and Germany constitute one of the essential elements of the consolidation of the situation in Europe and of the preservation of general peace. Consequently both Governments will endeavour with all their might to assure the development of the relations between their countries in this direction.

2) Both Governments agree that no question of a territorial nature remains in suspense between their countries and solemnly recognize as permanent the frontier between their countries as it is actually drawn.

---

[1] Published by the Ministère des Affaires Etrangères, *Documents Diplomatiques 1938-1939*, Paris, MDCCCCXXXIX. Doc. No. 28, p. 33.—*Ed.*

3) Both Governments are resolved, without prejudice to their special relations with third Powers, to remain in contact on all questions of importance to both their countries and to have recourse to mutual consultation in case any complications arising out of these questions should threaten to lead to international difficulties.

In witness whereof the Representatives of the two Governments have signed the present Declaration, which comes into force immediately.

Executed in duplicate in the French and German languages at Paris, on December 6, 1938.

Signed: *Georges Bonnet*
Joachim von Ribbentrop

No. 43

MINUTE OF A CONVERSATION BETWEEN THE CZECHOSLOVAK FOREIGN MINISTER CHVALKOVSKÝ AND THE BRITISH MINISTER IN PRAGUE NEWTON[1]

MINISTRY OF FOREIGN AFFAIRS

Cabinet No. 4265/38, Dec. 10, 1938

Translation
December 10, 1938

Secret

CONVERSATION BETWEEN FOREIGN MINISTER CHVALKOVSKÝ AND BRITISH MINISTER NEWTON

(Czech).[2] The Minister came to the Foreign Minister with a note (Depesche)[2] on the British attitude toward our circular note in which the Prague Government drew attention to the fact that we had carried out the Munich supplementary protocol, which was to be followed by a guarantee of our frontiers. On the instructions of his Government, the

---

[1] This document was seized by the Germans in the Archives of the Czechoslovak Foreign Ministry and translated by them into German. The document in the possession of the Archives Department of the Ministry of Foreign Affairs of the U.S.S.R. is the German translation found in the files of the German Foreign Ministry. It bears the stamp of the Political Archives of the German Foreign Ministry ("Pol. Arch.").—*Ed.*

[2] So in the original.—*Ed.*

Ministerium für Auswärtige Angelegenheiten.
Kabinett No 4265/38 vom 10.XII.1938.

Geheim

Übersetzung.

10.XII.1938.

Unterredung des Herrn Ministers Chvalkovský mit dem englischen Gesandten Newton.

(tschechisch) Der Gesandte kam mit einer Note (Depesche) über den englischen Standpunkt zu unserer Zirkulardepesche,in der die Prager Regierung darauf aufmerksam machte,daß wir das Münchener Ergänzungsprotokoll als Voraussetzung einer Grenzgarantie erfüllt hätten,zu dem Herrn Minister.Auf Weisung seiner Regierung teilte der Gesandte mit,daß die englische Regierung es sehr begrüßen würde,wenn wir selbst zur Frage der Garantie Stellung nehmen würden und besonders wenn wir erklären würden,wie wir uns die Garantie vorstellen. Die englischen Staatsmänner sprachen in Paris von einer generellen Garantie,aber sie haben nichts vereinbart.

(englisch) England beabsichtigte eine Art von gemeinsamer Garantie der Münchner Mächte.Die Engländer sind nicht darauf vorbereitet, eine Garantie zu geben,die sie nicht in Anwendung bringen könnten und sie würden sehr dankbar sein,wenn sie die Art der Garantie,die Prag im Auge hat,kennen würden.Sie haben von Berlin erfahren,daß Deutschland und Italien daran denken, eine unabhängige Garantie zu geben.Das würde natürlich für die Engländer sehr schwer sein,die gern den Wunsch der Prager Regierung,die Zusammenarbeit unter den vier Großmächten zu fördern,unterstützen würden,denn England befürchtet,daß die Achsenmächte diese Zusammenarbeit zwischen den westliche und den Zentralmächten aufspalten würden.Die Engländer könnten keine wirksame Garantie gegen die Zentralmächte geben,aber sie würden bereit sein eine Garantie zu geben,wenn wenigstens drei von den vieren zugunsten der Tschecho-Slowakei handeln würden.England wünscht keineswegs eine individuelle Garantie zu geben,d.h. nur eine gemeinsame mit zwei anderen Großmächten (dreien von vier),weil die Engländer sich nicht in die Lage Frankreichs vom vergangenen Oktober bringen würden.

Der tschecho-slowakische Minister antwortete:
1.) J e d e Art von Garantie würde willkommen sein und je weiter sie gehen würde, um so besser,

Photostatic copy of first page of Document No. 43

Minister stated that the British Government would very much welcome it if we ourselves were to state our views on the question of the guarantee, and especially if we explained how we conceived the guarantee. The British statesmen had discussed a general guarantee in Paris, but no agreement was reached.

(English).[1] Britain had in mind something in the nature of a joint guarantee of the Munich Powers. The British were not prepared to give a guarantee which they could not implement, and they would be very grateful to know what kind of guarantee Prague had in view. They had learned in Berlin that Germany and Italy were thinking of giving an independent guarantee. This, of course, would make it very difficult for the British, who would gladly support the desire of the Prague Government to promote collaboration between the four Great Powers, since Britain feared that the Axis Powers would frustrate collaboration between the Western and Central powers. The British could not give any effective guarantee against the Central Powers, but they would be prepared to give a guarantee if at least three of the four Powers acted in favour of Czechoslovakia. Britain had no desire to give an individual guarantee, but only one in conjunction with two other Great Powers (three out of the four), because the British would not put themselves in the position which France was in last October.

The Czechoslovak Foreign Minister replied:

1) *Any* kind of guarantee would be welcome, and the broader the better.

2) We would like to have this guarantee as soon as possible.

3) In reply to Newton's inquiry regarding a possible guarantee from other Powers besides the Munich Powers,

---

[1] So in the original.—*Ed.*

the Foreign Minister said the Czechoslovak Government had not yet considered such an eventuality, but the question would be taken under consideration as soon as the Munich Powers had mutually agreed on the guarantee.

(Czech).[1] In the course of the subsequent conversation, the British Minister repeatedly stressed the possibility that Czechoslovakia might be satisfied with a guarantee solely from Germany, which, in his opinion, was the most important, because Prague was probably aware how unwillingly Britain gave guarantees in cases where British interests were not directly affected, and still less willingly in cases, such as the present, where she had reason to doubt whether her guarantee would be of any use to us.

---

[1] So in the original.—*Ed.*

2.) daß wir wünschen würden, diese Garantie so bald als möglich zu haben.

3.) In Beantwortung von Newton's Frage über die eventuelle Garantie von anderen Mächten als denen von München, sagte der Minister, daß die tschecho-slowakische Regierung diese Eventualität noch nicht in Betracht gezogen hätte, daß aber die Frage sofort in Betracht gezogen werden würde, nachdem die Münchner Mächte in gegenseitiger Übereinstimmung die Garantie regeln würden.

(tschechisch) Im Verlauf der weiteren Unterhaltung legte der englische Gesandte einigemale Nachdruck auf die Möglichkeit, daß sich die Tschecho-Slowakei einzig und allein mit der Garantie Deutschlands zufrieden geben würde, die nach ihm die wichtigste ist, weil es angeblich Prag sicher bekannt sei, wie ungern England dort Garantien gebe, wo nicht direkt britische Interessen tangiert würden und noch weniger dort, wo – wie es gerade bei uns der Fall ist – sie berechtigte Zweifel hege, daß ihre Garantie uns etwas nützen würde.

F.d.R. *[signature]*

Photostatic copy of last page of Document No. 43

No. 44

LETTER FROM THE POLISH AMBASSADOR IN LONDON RACZYŃSKI TO THE POLISH AMBASSADOR IN BERLIN LIPSKI[1]

AMBASSADOR OF THE
POLISH REPUBLIC [2]

London, December 19, 1938

Ambassador Jozef Lipski,
    Berlin

Dear Jozef,

I take the liberty to enclose herewith a copy of a letter I sent to the Foreign Minister on the 16th inst.

I take advantage of the opportunity to convey my best wishes and heartiest congratulations on the occasion of the New Year. [3]

Yours,

Edward Raczyński

1 enclosure

---

[1] Original in Polish.
[2] Letterhead.
[3] The second paragraph and the signature are in Raczyński's own hand.—*Ed*.

ENCLOSURE

EMBASSY OF THE POLISH
REPUBLIC IN LONDON

London, December 16, 1938

No. 1/WB/257/tj/

Confidential

The Minister of Foreign Affairs,
Warsaw

Highly Esteemed Mr. Minister,

In view of the very abrupt changes that have taken place in the international situation and the reaction of certain States to these changes, to form any general conclusions is at the present moment a risky and thankless undertaking. Nevertheless, I consider it my duty to make the attempt, even if very sketchy, primarily with the object, Mr. Minister, of giving you a picture of the situation as one sees it from this local observation post. The only risk I take is that the picture, observed from a different angle, may seem tendentious or one-sided, or even just superficial or banal.

The post-Munich situation is assessed here as a state of neither war nor peace. Premier Chamberlain's assertion that a new era had come guaranteeing peace to "our generation" is considered by all to be an illusion, which contact with reality is causing swiftly to fade away. It must be

AMBASADOR RZECZYPOSPOLITEJ POLSKIEJ

Londyn, dnia 19 grudnia 1938r

Kochany Józiu

Pozwalam sobie przesłać Ci
w załączeniu odpis mojego listu wysłanego
do Pana Ministra Spraw Zagranicznych
w dniu 16 b.m.

JWielmożny Pan
  Ambasador Józef Lipski,
    w Berlinie.

1 zał.

Photostatic copy of accompanying letter to Document No. 44

Ambasada Rzeczypospolitej Polskiej
w Londynie.

N. 52/57/38

Londyn, dnia 16 grudnia 1938 r.

No.1/WB/257/tj

Tajne.

Wielce Szanowny Panie Ministrze,

Wobec nadzwyczaj gwałtownych zmian w położeniu międzynarodowym i reakcji na nie w poszczególnych państwach, wyciąganie wniosków ogólnych jest obecnie zadaniem ryzykownym i niewdzięcznym. Uważam pomimo to za swój obowiązek podjęcie takiej bardzo szkicowej próby, mając przedewszystkim na oku przedłożenie Panu Ministrowi obrazu sytuacji tak jak ona wygląda z tutejszego punktu obserwacyjnego. Ryzykuję tylko tyle, że widziany pod innym kątem widzenia, wydać się może tendencyjny lub jednostronny, o ile nie po prostu - ostrzony i banalny.

Sytuacja po-monachijska jest tutaj określana jako stan nie będący ani wojną ani też pokojem. Zapowiedzi premiera Chamberlaina o nastaniu nowej ery, gwarantującej pokój: " za naszego życia " oceniane są powszechnie jako iluzje, szybko rozwiewające się w zetknięciu z rzeczywistością. Trzeba przyznać, że p. Chamberlain z wielkim uporem i konsekwencją trzyma się obranej przez siebie linii, która ma go doprowadzić do Paktu Czterech i realizacji projektów " Nowej organizacji Europy ". Wartość

Do Pana Ministra
Spraw Zagranicznych,
w Warszawie.

admitted that Mr. Chamberlain is adhering very stubbornly and consistently to his chosen course, which is to lead to a four-power pact and the realization of the projects for a "new organization of Europe," based in one form or another on this pact. He continues to believe (honestly, I am assured) in the effectiveness of the method of personal contact between the responsible leaders of the partner States in the combination he has envisaged, and it is with this idea in mind that he is preparing for his next visit to Rome.

However, it is more than obvious that what is most attractive to the Englishman—"organization of Europe"—is not to the liking of Berlin, and that the realization of the rest of the Premier's program is proceeding very haltingly. So far the reply to his "active peace policy" has been three rude speeches by Hitler, the accentuation of the anti-Jewish course, as well as a new program of Italian claims, supported by Berlin.

One would think that, in view of such numerous disappointments, Mr. Chamberlain should be encountering increasing dissatisfaction and opposition not only in Parliament (where the opposition, thanks to party discipline, would not be so very effective), but above all among the British public. There is opposition, but, *mirabile dictu*, it apparently shows no signs of growth since Munich. I hear less about the likelihood of a Labour Party comeback than I did a year ago. True, from time to time there is talk of the formation of a real "National Government," to include both oppositions, but, as ever, without conviction.

For all this there are various reasons, of which two seem to me the most important.

First: *The general opinion is that "Munich" was the most correct, if not the only, way out of a desperate situation.* [1]

---

[1] Underscored in the original.—*Ed*.

I recently heard some characteristic remarks from a high official in the Foreign Office, who is known for his critical attitude toward the Premier's policy. This gentleman agreed with the above opinion, only with the reservation that the Premier made a big mistake when he said that peace purchased at such a price was a "peace with honour."[1] For that matter, the Premier himself is said to regret this expression, which he used under the stress of deep emotion.

(Furthermore, my informer asserted that the Western States were able to "wriggle out of an extremely difficult situation without war thanks to the decision of the Czechs to capitulate without a fight. . . .[2])

Second: The conviction that the Premier (to draw a not very exact parallel with the field of sports) blocked the British goal, and thus carried the game into the East of Europe. Whatever happens, the fact remains that time has been gained. And adjournment[3] is no less popular in this home of political empiricism than in Geneva.

It is hard for me to fathom what the Premier is thinking, and whether he is less naive, or less sincere, than they say he is. But on the other hand I do know, on the basis of long observation, the reaction of the folk here. It is as vital, spontaneous, uniform, almost physiological, as the reaction of ants and bees, and is independent of the phraseology with which public opinion here is regularly fed. Notwithstanding all the talk of the active elements of the opposition, a conflict in Eastern Europe which threatens in one way or another to embroil Germany and Russia is *universally and subconsciously regarded*

---

[1] The words "peace with honour" are in English in the original.—*Ed*.

[2] The inverted commas are not closed in the original.—*Ed*.

[3] The word "adjournment" is in English.—*Ed*.

here as a "lesser evil" capable of deferring the menace to the Empire and its overseas components for a longer period. [1]

Chamberlain's attitude to the Soviets continues to be cold. The truth is that he is extremely consistent and quite frankly avoids everything that might serve as an excuse or pretext to his political partners to decline to collaborate. But the truth also is that the Premier officially is particularly careful to avoid doing anything to oppose Germany's designs in the East.

The British public are at last realizing with satisfaction that the Premier's policy does not mean a renunciation of rearmament—on the contrary, thanks to the respite it makes rearmament possible. [2]

As the above remarks will show, Mr. Nèville Chamberlain, in spite of the disappointments and even humiliating unpleasantness he meets with, continues to remain a "force" in British politics.

On the other hand, he is being very bitterly criticized not only by the opposition (who accuse him of being guided not only by national, but also class interests, in the Spanish question for instance), but also by political "experts," and primarily by his own officials. [3]

In those quarters it is now asserted that even if the general lines of his policy are correct (or furnish a good excuse for a respite), his tactics are unfortunate. I might again cite the opinion of two high officials who told me that they are well aware how low the prestige of the Premier

---

[1] Underscored in the original.—*Ed.*

[2] Although still one-sided, of which I shall speak presently.—*Raczyński's note.*

[3] This is also indicative of how far the Premier has gone in removing the officials from the making of foreign policy.—*Raczyński's note.*

has fallen in Germany, where only quite recently he enjoyed great respect. . . . What his officials want today is not a radical change of the system, but greater persistence at its various stages—that no political or economic positions in Europe should be voluntarily surrendered in the illusory hope of securing in return a more indulgent or yielding attitude elsewhere.

Lastly, there is still another important field where opinions differ. This is the question of national defence. Premier Chamberlain has to this day not abandoned the platform of retaining voluntary military service and at the same time pushing the expansion of the navy and the air force, without, however, taking measures to create a land army capable of offensive operations. The Premier's restraint may be explained by his well-known tendency to conciliate the militaristic Axis powers. On the other hand, in view of the approaching elections he has to reckon with the unpopularity of conscription in Britain, especially among the workers. The officials, however, want conscription. It is also ardently desired by the "patriotic" opposition. Its introduction, which could take place if at all only after the elections, would be the most eloquent proof that Britain is passing from an attitude of mild conciliation to increased "firmness."

I may be mistaken, but my belief is not only that such a turn must take place, but that the beginnings of such a turn are already in evidence. They take the form of changes, so far inconspicuous, in the character of official pronouncements. I also refer to the extension of the system which permits the government to guarantee credits granted by industrialists to foreign clients, and also the first attempt to extend such guarantees to war materials (so far they are confined to the £10,000,000 sanctioned last week by the House of Commons on the motion of the government).

Such is the background against which the attitude of the English toward Poland should be judged. As to the Premier, his friends and his press, there is no doubt that here we are meeting with great reserve.

The post-Munich ice has been broken, personal prejudices are being forgotten; however, a reluctance still prevails to make commitments, especially such as might be given an anti-German construction. The Foreign Office has so far only ventured the following admission, made to me in friendly conversation: "The British Government certainly does not want Poland to abandon the balance of power policy pursued till now" (Strang, December 9).

Meanwhile, I must note that for some time there has been something in the nature of an organized campaign among the public and the press here, using lurid news stories and even downright gossip and insinuation to represent Polish-German relations in an unfavourable light. [1]

This state of affairs gives rise to alarm and pessimistic opinions as to Poland's political position. The above-mentioned "drive"—if one may speak of a drive in this case, of which there is no clear evidence—is primarily developing around the problem of Transcarpathian Rus and the claims on the Ukraine, but at the same time it is extended to other possible causes of friction, such as Danzig, and lately (*Daily Express* and even the *Times*), even Teschen Silesia, from which, through Prague or Moravská Ostrava, serious disturbances were reported in the press. [2]

---

[1] In order to be exact, I must emphasize that Rumania is the subject of perhaps even more alarmist comments. Incidentally, the Rumanians here are very uneasy about it.—*Raczyński's note*.

[2] This latter gossip is perhaps a countermeasure on the part of Prague in revenge for Transcarpathian Rus.—*Raczyński's note*.

It is difficult here to counteract the press, unless you meet with overt misrepresentations of the facts which can be denied (as we are, of course, constantly doing). A more effective method might be to operate with positive facts "from the spot" which would *implicite* refute the circulated gossip. It need not be said that such machinations are prejudicial to our political prestige and credit here, especially just now, when England is only gradually beginning to throw off the fetters of defeatism.

>
> Accept, etc.,
>
> *Edward Raczyński*

NAME INDEX*

ALTENBURG GÜNTHER: German diplomatist; appointed to the rank of Minister in 1939; head of Sub-section IVb (Czechoslovakia) in the Political Department of the German Foreign Office, 1938-39; appointed head of the Information Department of the Foreign Office, August 21, 1939.— 93, 99, 169, 275

ASHTON-GWATKIN, FRANK: British diplomatist; Counsellor at Foreign Office, 1934. Was sent to Czechoslovakia with Lord Runciman's mission in 1938.—156, 159, 160, 264-266

BALBO, ITALO: Italian Minister of Aviation, 1929-33.—149, 155

BAXTER, C. W.: British diplomatist; acting Counsellor in Foreign Office.—92

BECK, JOZEF: Polish diplomatist; Minister of Foreign Affairs, 1932-39.—145, 176, **219**, 226

BENEŠ, EDUARD: **Czechoslovak** Foreign Minister, 1918-35; President of the **Czechoslovak** Republic, 1935-38; head of the Czechoslovak National Committee in Paris, 1939-40; again elected President of the Czechoslovak Republic, July 1940.— 46, 95, 108, 146, 152, 156, 159, 160, 202, 204, 223

BÉRENGER, HENRI: Chairman of the Foreign Affairs Committee of the French Senate, 1931-38; Delegate to the League of Nations, 1932-38.—74-80

BEST, WERNER: Chief of the "Legal" Department of the Gestapo and close collaborator of Himmler.—164, 167, 168

BLUM, LÉON: Right Socialist, leader of the French Socialist Party; Prime Minister of France, 1936-37; Vice-Premier, 1937-38; Prime Minister and Minister of Finance, March-April, 1938.—126

---

* The data given in the index, as a rule, relates to the period when the given person is mentioned in the documents.

BONNET, GEORGES: French Minister of Foreign Affairs in the Daladier Cabinet, 1938-39.—107, 109, 110, 113-121, 139, 284, 285

BRIAND, ARISTIDE: French Prime Minister and Minister of Foreign Affairs, November 1925-July 1926, and again in 1929; Minister of Foreign Affairs, 1928-32.—90, 91

BULLITT, WILLIAM CHRISTIAN: American Ambassador to France, 1936-40, known for his connections with the Hitlerites.—121

CADOGAN, Sir ALEXANDER: British diplomatist; Deputy Under Secretary of State at Foreign Office, 1936-37; Permanent Under Secretary of State for Foreign Affairs, 1938-46.—100, 103, 104

CAILLAUX, JOSEPH: Prime Minister of France, 1911-12; Senator; several times Minister of Finance; Chairman of Senate Finance Committee in 1932-38.—74

ČERMÁK, VLASTIMIL: Czechoslovak diplomatist; Minister to Albania, 1934.—269

CHAMBERLAIN, NEVILLE: Leader of the British Conservative Party; big capitalist; Prime Minister, 1937-40.—40, 44, 51, 55, 58, 62, 82-85, 107, 108, 125, 127-131, 145, 149, 165, 179, 181, 183, 184, 193, 211-213, 215, 217, 218, 220, 223, 224, 229, 235-240, 250, 256, 259, 263, 265-267, 270, 271, 294, 299, 301, 302

CHAUTEMPS, CAMILLE: Member of the French Chamber of Deputies since 1919; Prime Minister, 1937-38; Vice-Premier, March-July, 1940.—74

CHURCHILL, WINSTON SPENCER: Leader of the British Conservative Party; from 1937 to 1939 held no government post; First Lord of Admiralty, 1939-40; Prime Minister, 1940-45.—128, 135

CHVALKOVSKÝ, FRANTIŠEK KAREL: Czechoslovak Minister of Foreign Affairs since December 1, 1938; together with Hácha signed the act of March 15, 1939, liquidating Czechoslovakia's independence.—286

COMNEN (see PETRESCU)

DALADIER, ÉDOUARD: A leader of the French Radical-Socialist Party; Minister of National Defence and Vice-Premier, 1936-37; Prime Minister, Minister of National Defence and Minister of Foreign Affairs, 1938-40.—107, 108, 172, 237, 238, 240, 250, 259, 260, 263, 266, 267, 270

DELBOS, YVON: A leader of the French Radical-Socialist Party; Minister of Foreign Affairs, 1936-37; and in March-April, 1938.—70, 73, 74, 79

DEMBIŃSKI: Director of the Polish Telegraph Agency.—220

DIRKSEN, HERBERT von: German diplomatist; big landowner; Ambassador to Moscow, November 1928-August 1933; Ambassador to Japan, September 1933-February 1938; Ambassador to England, March 31, 1938-September 3, 1939.—122, 132

EDEN, ROBERT ANTHONY: British Conservative leader; Secretary of State for Foreign Affairs, 1935-38; Secretary of State for Dominion Affairs, 1939; Secretary of State for War, 1940, and Secretary of State for Foreign Affairs in Churchill's Cabinet, 1940-45.—41, 69, 127, 128

EISENLOHR, ERNST: German diplomatist; Minister to Greece, 1931-36; to Czechoslovakia, 1936-39.—46, 86, 88, 93, 99

FAUCHER, LOUIS: General; Chief of the French Military Mission in Czechoslovakia in 1938.—171

FIERLINGER, ZDENĚK: Director of the Political Department of the Czechoslovak Foreign Office, 1935-37; Minister to Moscow, 1937-39; Ambassador to Moscow, 1941-45; Prime Minister, 1945-46.—171, 203

FLANDIN, PIERRE ÉTIENNE: French Prime Minister, November 1934-June 1935; Minister of Foreign Affairs, January-June, 1936.—69, 70, 73, 74

FOERSTER, ALBERT: Nazi leader in Danzig.—135, 136, 138

FRANÇOIS-PONCET, ANDRÉ: French diplomatist; Ambassador to Germany, 1931-38; Ambassador to Rome, 1938.—230

FRANK, KARL HERMANN: Henlein's deputy as leader of the Nazi Sudeten German Party; after the German occupation of Czechoslovakia, Secretary of State of the "Protectorate Bohemia-Moravia" under Reichsprotector Neurath; tried as war criminal by Czechoslovak court and executed in 1946.—86, 88, 99, 195, 196

FRANZONI, FRANCESCO: Italian diplomatist; Counsellor in the Italian Embassy to Brazil, 1926; Minister to Lithuania, 1935.—270

GAMELIN, MARIE GUSTAVE: French General; Chief of General Staff, 1931-39; Commander-in-Chief of the French Army, 1939-40—110, 116-118, 171

GLAISE von HORSTENAU, EDMUND: Minister Without Portfolio in Schuschnigg Cabinet since July 1936; Austrian Minister of Interior, November 1936-March 1938.—83

GOERING, HERMANN: Major German war criminal; Commander of Military Air Corps and Minister for Air; Commissar for carrying out the "Four-Year-Plan"; sentenced to death by the International Military Tribunal in 1946.—64, 81-85, 117, 149-152, 155

HALIFAX, EDWARD, Viscount: British Secretary of State for War, 1935; Minister Without Portfolio (Lord Privy Seal), 1935-37; Secretary of State for Foreign Affairs, 1938-40.—13, 14, 19, 23, 29, 31, 33, 40, 41, 44, 45, 50, 51, 60, 82-85, 104, 125, 129, 131, 217

HAUSHOFER, KARL, Professor: President of the German Academy in Munich; editor of Nazi journal *Zeitschrift für Geopolitik*; leading member of the Central Office of the Volksdeutsche.—99

HENCKE, A.: German diplomatist; Chargé d'Affaires in Czechoslovakia, September 1938.—268

HENDERSON, Sir NEVILE: British diplomatist; Ambassador to Germany, 1937-39.—50, 52, 62-64, 104, 146

HENLEIN, KONRAD: Head of the Nazi party in the Sudeten region of Czechoslovakia originally known as the Sudetendeutsche Heimatfront and from 1935 as the Sudetendeutsche Partei; after the dismemberment of Czechoslovakia appointed Reichskommissar and later Reichsstathalter of the Sudetenland.—86, 94, 95, 99, 103, 108, 136, 156, 159, 160, 172, 194-196, 198

HEYDEN-RYNSCH: Official, with rank of Legationsrat, of Sub-department I (League of Nations, military affairs, armament, etc.) of Political Department of German Foreign Office, 1938-39; officer for liaison with the Oberkommando of the Wehrmacht; Counsellor to the German Embassy in Madrid, from 1941.—167

HIMMLER, HEINRICH: Major German war criminal; Reichsführer SS; Chief of German Police.—167, 169

- HITLER, ADOLF: Head of the German fascists; Chancellor of the Reich and "Führer," 1933-45.—13, 50, 108, 116, 136-138, 152, 155, 163, 173, 175, 176, 191, 195, 211-213, 215, 217, 218, 223-225, 250, 265, 271, 299

- HODŽA, MILAN, Dr.: Prime Minister of Czechoslovakia, November 1935-September 1938.—87, 95, 103, 202

- HOHENLOHE, MORITZ, Prince: Was close to ruling circles of Hitler Germany; acted as intermediary in the negotiations of Runciman and Ashton-Gwatkin with Henlein in August 1938.—156, 160

- HORE-BELISHA, LESLIE: Parliamentary Secretary to the British Board of Trade, 1931-32; Financial Secretary to the Treasury, 1932-34; Minister of Transport, 1934-37; Secretary of State for War, 1937-40.—131

- HORTHY, NIKOLAUS, Admiral: Regent of Hungary, 1920-44; took active part in suppressing the Hungarian revolution of 1919; leader of Szegedin counter-revolutionary movement; Hungary began war on the U.S.S.R. (1941) during his regency.—150, 151, 182

- IMRÉDY, BÉLA: Hungarian banker; Governor of National Bank, 1935-38; Prime Minister, 1938-39; Minister Without Portfolio, 1944; in 1940, founded the fascist Hungarian Renovation Party and was its leader until the liberation of Hungary by the Soviet Army; executed as war criminal in 1946.—176

- INA: General Secretary of the Czechoslovak Foreign Ministry, with rank of Minister in 1938.—268

- JURY: Minister of Social Welfare in the Nazi Seyss-Inquart Government, in 1938.—83

- KEITEL, WILHELM: General; Major German war criminal; official in the War Ministry, 1935-38; from 1938 till the defeat of Hitler Germany, Chief of Staff of the Oberkommando of the Wehrmacht. Field-Marshal from 1941; executed in 1946 by sentence of the International Military Tribunal.—272, 275

- KELLOGG, FRANK BILLINGS: Secretary of State of the U.S.A., 1925-29.—90, 91

- KORDT, ERICH: German diplomatist; Counsellor in the Foreign Office, 1939-40.—99, 256, 263

- KREISSL: A leader of the Sudeten German Party in Czechoslovakia.—99

KRNO, IVAN, Dr.: Official of the Czechoslovak Foreign Office with rank of Minister.—269

KROFTA, KAMIL: Minister of Foreign Affairs of the Czechoslovak Republic, 1936-38.—46, 68, 100, 104, 140, 171, 268, 269

KÜNZEL: A leader of the Sudeten German Party; Henlein's representative in Berlin, 1938.—99

LACROIX, LÉOPOLD-VICTOR de: French diplomatist; Minister to Czechoslovakia, 1936-39.—269

LAMMERS, HEINRICH: Nazi civil servant; Secretary of State in the Reich Chancellery, 1933-37; Reichsminister and Head of Reich Chancellery from 1937 to downfall of Hitler Germany.—163

LAVAL, PIERRE: French Minister of Foreign Affairs, 1934-35; Prime Minister and Minister of Foreign Affairs, 1935-36; actually a Nazi agent; executed in 1946 by sentence of a French court.—79

LÉGER, ALEXIS: French diplomatist; General Secretary for Foreign Affairs, 1933-40.—70, 266, 267

LIPSKI, JOZEF: Polish diplomatist; Ambassador to Berlin, 1934-39.—145, 155, 176, 184, 219, 225, 226, 231, 293

LITVINOV, MAXIM MAXIMOVICH: People's Commissar of Foreign Affairs of the U.S.S.R., 1930-39.—89, 92

LORENZ, WERNER: SS Obergruppenführer; one of the leading members of the Central Office of the Volksdeutsche.—99

LUKASIEWICZ, JULJUSZ: Polish diplomatist; Ambassador to U.S.S.R., 1933-36; Ambassador to France, 1936-39.—109

MACDONALD, JAMES RAMSAY: Leader of the British Labour Party; National-Labourist since 1931; Prime Minister and Secretary of State for Foreign Affairs, 1924; Prime Minister, 1929-35.—32, 109

MACKENSEN, HANS GEORG von: German diplomatist; Minister to Hungary, 1933-37; Secretary of State at Foreign Office, 1937-38; Ambassador to Italy, 1938-43.—99

MASARYK, JAN: Czechoslovak diplomatist; Minister to Great Britain, 1925-39.—100, 104, 136, 172, 202, 217, 218

MASAŘIK, HUBERT: Official of the Czechoslovak Foreign Office, 1938.—264

MASSIGLI, RENÉ: French diplomatist; Chief of League of Nations Section at Ministry of Foreign Affairs, 1928-29; Assistant Director of Political Section at Ministry of Foreign Affairs, 1933-37; director of this section, 1937-38.—70

MASTNÝ, ADALBERT: Czechoslovak diplomatist; Minister to Germany, 1932-39.—265-67

MILLERAND, ALEXANDRE: French Minister of War, 1914-15; General-Commissioner in Alsace-Lorraine, 1919; Prime Minister, 1920; President of the Republic, 1920-24.—80

MUSSOLINI, BENITO: Chief of the Italian fascists; Premier and virtual dictator of Italy, 1922-43; executed by Italian patriots in 1945.—155, 224, 250, 263

NEURATH, KONSTANTIN von: Major German war criminal; Minister of Foreign Affairs, 1932-38; Reichsprotector of Bohemia and Moravia, 1939-43; sentenced by International Military Tribunal to fifteen years' imprisonment.—13-15, 40, 46, 49, 51

NEWTON, Sir BASIL: British diplomatist; Minister to Czechoslovakia, December 1936-39.—103, 104, 211, 213-216, 270, 286, 289

NIEMÖLLER, MARTIN: German Protestant pastor; arrested by the Nazis in 1937.—125

NOÉ, LUDWIG: Foerster's interpreter during his conversation with Winston Churchill in July 1938.—136

OSUSKÝ, ŠTEFAN: Czechoslovak diplomatist; Minister to France, 1920-39.—68, 80, 171

PAPEN, FRANZ von: Major German war criminal; Reich Chancellor, May 30, 1932-January 30, 1933; Nazi Special Ambassador to Austria, 1934-38; Ambassador to Turkey, 1939-44.—63

PARIANI, ALBERTO: Chief of Italian General Staff, 1936-39.—155

PAUL-BONCOUR, JOSEPH: French Prime Minister and Minister of Foreign Affairs, December 1932-Janury 1933; Minister of Foreign Affairs, January 1933-February 1934.—103

PETRESCU-COMNEN: Rumanian diplomatist; Minister to Berlin, 1932-38.—139, 140, 149

POTEMKIN, VLADIMIR P.: Vice-Commissar of Foreign Affairs of the U.S.S.R., 1937-40.—203

RACZYŃSKI, EDWARD, Count: Polish diplomatist; Ambassador to Great Britain, 1934-39.—293, 301, 303, 304

REYNAUD, PAUL: French industrialist and politician; several times Minister of Finance and Minister of Justice; Minister of Finance, November 1939-March 1940.—69, 70

RIBBENTROP, JOACHIM von: Major German war criminal; Ambassador to Great Britain, 1936-38; Reichsminister of Foreign Affairs from February 1938 to downfall of Hitler Germany; executed by sentence of the International Military Tribunal in 1946.—50, 52, 61, 63, 67, 81-85, 93, 94, 96, 97, 99, 176, 181, 183, 184, 219, 220, 223-226, 229-231, 284, 285

RIPKA, HUBERT: Czechoslovak journalist.—187, 191, 211, 264

RITTER, KARL: German diplomatist; as head of the Economic Department at the Ministry of Foreign Affairs in 1930-35, he took part in political and economic negotiations with Belgium, Poland, Finland and France; Ambassador to Brazil in 1937-38, after which worked in Foreign Office.—279

ROCHAT, M.: French diplomatist; Chef de Cabinet at the Foreign Office.—70, 264, 267

RUNCIMAN, WALTER, Lord: National-Liberal Party; President of the British Board of Trade, 1931-37; Lord President of the Council, 1938-39; the head of the British Mission sent to Czechoslovakia in 1938.—145, 146, 149-152, 156, 159, 160, 173, 193, 202

RYDZ-SMIGLY, EDWARD: Marshal of Poland; successor to Pilsudski; Inspector-General of the Armed Forces, 1938-39.—117, 118

SANDER, FRITZ: Professor of law at the German University in Prague.—159

SANDYS, DUNCAN: British Conservative and Member of Parliament.—128, 131

SCHACHT, HJALMAR: Major German war criminal; President of the Reichsbank, 1923-30; 1933-39.—13-15

SCHMIDT, GUIDO: Austrian Secretary of State in the Ministry of Foreign Affairs, 1936-38; Minister of Foreign Affairs in Schuschnigg Cabinet, 1938.—63, 67

SCHUSCHNIGG, KURT von: Leader of the Austrian Christian Social Party; Chancellor of the Austrian Republic, 1934-38.—82, 83

SEYSS-INQUART, ARTHUR: Austrian Hitlerite; Minister of the Interior and Public Security in Schuschnigg Cabinet, February-March, 1938; after the Anschluss, Governor of the Austrian Gau of the Hitler Reich.—82, 83

SIMON, Sir JOHN: National-Liberal Party; British Secretary of State for Foreign Affairs, 1931-35; Secretary of State for Home Affairs, 1935-37; Chancellor of the Exchequer, 1937-40.—41

SMUTNÝ, I.: General Secretary to President of the Czechoslovak Republic Beneš, 1935-38.—211, 214, 216, 269

STECHOW, von: Vice-Consul; Official in Nazi Ministry of Foreign Affairs, 1938-39.—165, 166

STIEVE, FRIEDRICH: German diplomatist; director of the "Cultural Political" Department of the Foreign Office, 1933-39.—99

STRANG, Sir WILLIAM: British diplomatist; Counsellor in Foreign Office; director of the Central Europe Department, 1938-39.—303

STRESEMANN, GUSTAV: German Reich Chancellor and Minister of Foreign Affairs, 1923; Minister of Foreign Affairs, 1923-29.—118

SWINTON, Sir PHILIP: British Secretary of State for Colonies, 1931-35; Secretary of State for Air, 1935-38.—128,131

SYROVÝ, JAN, General: Inspector-General of the Czechoslovak Forces; Prime Minister of Czechoslovakia, September 22-December 1, 1938.—269

SZEMBEK, JAN, Count: Polish Vice-Minister of Foreign Affairs, 1932-39.—149

SZTOJAY, DOEME: Hungarian officer and diplomatist; Military Attaché in Berlin, 1925-33; Minister to Germany, 1935-44; Prime Minister of Hungarian puppet government, March-August 1944.—151

TWARDOWSKI, von: German diplomatist; Counsellor to Embassy in Moscow, 1929-35; Deputy Director of the "Cultural Political" Department of the Foreign Office, 1936-39.—99

VANSITTART, Sir ROBERT: Permanent Under Secretary of State for Foreign Affairs, 1930-38; Chief Diplomatic Adviser to Foreign Secretary, 1938-41.—60, 61

VOROSHILOV, KLEMENT EFREMOVICH: Marshal of the Soviet Union; People's Commissar of Military and Naval Affairs of the U.S.S.R., 1925-34; People's Commissar of Defence of the U.S.S.R., 1934-40.—58

WEIZSÄCKER, ERNST, Baron von: German diplomatist; Director of Political Department of Foreign Office, 1936-38; Secretary of State at Foreign Office, 1938-43.—86, 93, 99, 219, 223, 224, 226, 229, 230, 272, 276

WELCZEK, JOHANNES, Count von: German diplomatist; Ambassador to Spain, 1926-36; to France, 1936-39.—230

WELLES, SUMNER: United States Under Secretary of State, 1937-43.—121

WILSON, WOODROW: President of the U.S.A., 1912-20; Head of the American Delegation at the Peace Conference in Paris, 1919.—57, 59

WILSON, Sir HORACE: Close collaborator of Neville Chamberlain; Chief Industrial Adviser to the British Government, 1930-39; Permanent Secretary of the Treasury and Head of the Civil Service, 1939-42; one of the few advisers of Chamberlain during his negotiations with Hitler in September 1938; in the summer of 1939 conducted in Chamberlain's name secret negotiations with the Germans for a broad Anglo-German agreement.—225, 226, 229, 231, 265, 266

WILSON, HUGH ROBERT: American diplomatist; Ambassador to Germany, March 1938-December 1941.—146, 149

WINTERTON, EDWARD, Earl: British Minister Without Portfolio (Chancellor of Duchy of Lancaster), 1937-39; Under Secretary of State for Air, 1938; Under Secretary of State for Home Affairs, 1938.—128, 131

WOERMANN, ERNST: German diplomatist; Director of Political Department and Under Secretary of State at Foreign Office, 1938-43.—139, 140, 169, 170, 205, 206, 224